THE WEEKL

Vegan Meal Plan

COOKBOOK

THE WEEKLY
Vegan Meal Plan
COOKBOOK

A **3-MONTH** KICKSTART GUIDE
TO **PLANT-BASED COOKING**

Kylie Perrotti

author of *The Weekly Meal Plan Cookbook*

Skyhorse Publishing

Skyhorse Publishing books may be purchased in bulk at special discounts for sales promotion, corporate gifts, fund-raising, or educational purposes. Special editions can also be created to specifications. For details, contact the Special Sales Department, Skyhorse Publishing, 307 West 36th Street, 11th Floor, New York, NY 10018 or info@skyhorsepublishing.com.

Skyhorse® and Skyhorse Publishing® are registered trademarks of Skyhorse Publishing, Inc.®, a Delaware corporation.

Visit our website at www.skyhorsepublishing.com.

10 9 8 7 6 5 4 3 2 1

Library of Congress Cataloging-in-Publication Data is available on file.

Cover design by Mumtaz Mustafa
Cover photo by Kylie Perrotti

Print ISBN: 978-1-5107-6465-1
Ebook ISBN: 978-1-5107-6466-8

Printed in China

This book is dedicated to my parents, Jim and Barbara Thompson, who continue to cheer me on; my husband, Jason Perrotti, for being a supportive partner and a very honest taste-tester; and my cat, Grammy, for being the friendliest and furriest sous chef. I also owe a great deal of gratitude to my friends of the Baltimore Supper Club who inspire me daily with their passion for food and cooking.

Contents

Introduction

I am a self-taught home cook who started a recipe blog (TriedAndTrueRecipe.com) because I wanted a no-frills, no-nonsense approach to finding easy, elegant, and delicious meals to make at home. From my growing catalog of recipes, I created my first book, *The Weekly Meal Plan Cookbook*, a cookbook for people who don't want to fuss with meal planning. My books are made for anyone wanting to elevate their cooking but not wanting to go through the trouble of buying ingredients and struggling to find other recipes that call for those same ingredients throughout the week. These meal plans have been crafted to overlap a week's worth of ingredients before they must go into the garbage can.

The goal of this book is to take the guesswork out of planning with a comprehensive grocery list (organized by department, of course!), reusable, easy-to-source, accessible ingredients, and simple recipes for beginner home cooks. Can't find an ingredient? No problem. The trickier ingredients come with substitution suggestions. Many of the vegetables also come with substitution suggestions, so if your grocery store is out of golden beets, I got you covered.

This book is focused exclusively on plant-forward recipes. It does not subscribe to the whole-foods, plant-based diet, but there are suggestions throughout the weekly meal plans for replacing processed grains with whole grains. Every recipe is 100 percent vegan.

PLAN 1: WEEK 1

This recipe plan includes dinner recipes for five days, all of which serve four. To conquer the grocery store in one shopping trip, the next page outlines a detailed grocery list, with items separated by store department. You will also find storage, freezing, and thawing tips to help you plan your week. This plan is all about flavor-laden broths and sauces to elevate simple ingredients. Pay special attention to the key players throughout the week (shitake mushrooms, baby kale, and shallots) and be sure to buy the freshest and healthiest of those ingredients that you can find, because you will use them for multiple recipes.

THE MENU

MONDAY
Easy White Miso Brothy Beans

TUESDAY
Braised Tatsoi with Crispy Tofu

WEDNESDAY
Sweet Potato Fritters with Harissa Sour Cream

THURSDAY
Vegan Coconut Curry Soba with Mushrooms

FRIDAY
Balsamic Farro Salad with Figs

1

PLAN 1: WEEK 1

CONQUERING THE GROCERY STORE

FOOD SAFETY GUIDELINES

Buying groceries for the entire week can require some forethought, so be sure to refer to the FDA's storage and freezing guidelines for your ingredients. To keep herbs and leafy greens fresh through the week, wrap them in a damp paper towel and store in a bag in your crisper. Refresh the paper towel periodically through the week to keep them extra fresh.

PLANT-BASED PROTEIN

☐ 1 pound extra-firm tofu

☐ Liquid egg substitute

GRAINS

☐ 1 cup farro

OIL

☐ Avocado oil

☐ Extra-virgin olive oil

PLANT-BASED DAIRY

☐ ½ cup plant-based sour cream

STOCK

☐ 14 cups vegetable stock

FRUITS & VEGETABLES

☐ 5 shallots

☐ 10 ounces shitake mushrooms

☐ 8 ounces cremini mushrooms

☐ 4 ounces maitake or oyster mushrooms

☐ 1 pound sweet potatoes

☐ 1 head garlic

☐ 3 teaspoons or 1 (1-inch) piece of ginger

☐ 1 head tatsoi

☐ 10 ounces baby kale

☐ 10 ounces fresh green beans

☐ 3 Thai chili peppers

☐ 4 Roma tomatoes

☐ 1 pint cherry tomatoes

☐ 4 ounces pomegranate seeds

☐ 1 lime

☐ 1 lemon

☐ 1 pint figs

☐ 2 ounces basil leaves

☐ ½ cup fresh parsley leaves

☐ ½ ounce mint

☐ 6 scallions

PANTRY & SPICES

- [ ] 2 (15-ounce) cans cannellini beans
- [ ] 1 (15-ounce) can coconut milk
- [ ] ⅓ cup roasted, unsalted peanuts
- [ ] 16 ounces soba noodles
- [ ] Star anise pods
- [ ] Chinese cooking wine
- [ ] Soy sauce
- [ ] Pure sesame oil
- [ ] Cassava flour
- [ ] White miso paste
- [ ] Harissa powder
- [ ] All-purpose flour
- [ ] Curry powder
- [ ] Turmeric
- [ ] Cayenne powder
- [ ] Sesame seeds
- [ ] Balsamic vinegar
- [ ] Maple syrup
- [ ] Dijon mustard
- [ ] Flaky sea salt
- [ ] Salt
- [ ] Pepper

Easy White Miso Brothy Beans

Time to Make: 25 minutes

Serves: 4

WHY THIS RECIPE WORKS

Fast, filling, and healthy, this recipe combines sweetly acidic tomatoes with the complex umami flavor of white miso and the richness of creamy white beans.

SUBSTITUTIONS

Shallots: Try this with Vidalia/yellow onions or sliced leeks
Roma tomatoes: Canned, whole peeled, or diced tomatoes
Cannellini beans: Any canned white bean, such as navy or great northern

EQUIPMENT & LEFTOVERS

You'll need: Wide pot
Leftovers: Store in an airtight container in the fridge for 3 days

INGREDIENTS

2 teaspoons avocado oil
2 shallots, peeled and quartered
4 Roma tomatoes, quartered
2 tablespoons white miso paste
4 cups vegetable stock
Salt and pepper to taste
2 (15-ounce) cans cannellini beans, drained
½ cup fresh parsley, minced, plus more for garnish

METHOD

1. **Cook the shallots:** Heat the avocado oil in a wide pot over medium heat. Add the shallots and cook for 1 minute until just beginning to sweat.

2. **Char the tomatoes:** Place the tomatoes in an even layer in the pot. Ensure that they are cut-side down. Turn the heat to high and cook for 3 to 4 minutes until the tomatoes and shallots begin to char.

3. **Brown the miso paste:** Reduce heat to medium and add the miso paste into an open spot in the pot and mash it into the pot with a spoon. Cook for 45 seconds until it begins to brown slightly.

4. **Pour in the vegetable stock:** Whisk the miso into the broth until completely combined. Taste and season with salt and pepper.

5. **Simmer the brothy beans:** Add the beans and bring to a boil. Boil for five minutes until the broth reduces slightly. Reduce heat to low and simmer for 10 minutes. Add the parsley and stir to combine.

6. **To serve:** Ladle the broth into bowls and garnish with more parsley. Enjoy!

Braised Tatsoi with Crispy Tofu

Time to Make: 55 minutes (25 minutes inactive)

Serves: 4

WHY THIS RECIPE WORKS

A clean, aromatic broth paired with crispy tofu and tatsoi, this recipe gets its textural contrast from crunchy peanuts and shallots piled on top.

SUBSTITUTIONS

Shallot: Small yellow onion
Shitake mushrooms: Any mushroom variety, such as cremini, baby bella, oyster, or maitake
Star anise pods: ½ teaspoon Chinese Five Spice powder
Cassava flour: Arrowroot powder, tapioca flour, or coconut flour
Tatsoi: Baby bok choy or spinach; if using spinach, only cook for 3 to 4 minutes until wilted
Peanuts: Cashews or almonds
Thai chili peppers: Your favorite hot pepper, such as habanero, jalapeño, or serrano

EQUIPMENT & LEFTOVERS

You'll need: Paper towels, heavy object to press tofu, wide pot, and small skillet
Leftovers: Store in an airtight container in the fridge for 3 days

INGREDIENTS

1 pound extra-firm tofu
3 teaspoons avocado oil, divided
2 shallots, peeled and sliced into thin wedges, divided
6 ounces shitake mushrooms, stems removed and caps thinly sliced
6 cloves garlic, peeled and minced
2 star anise pods
6 scallions, minced, divided
¼ cup Chinese cooking wine
1 tablespoon soy sauce
2 teaspoons pure sesame oil, divided
4 cups vegetable stock
1 teaspoon salt plus more to taste
½ teaspoon pepper plus more to taste
1 head tatsoi
⅓ cup cassava flour
1 teaspoon sesame oil
⅓ cup roasted, unsalted peanuts, lightly crushed
1–2 Thai chili peppers, thinly sliced
Flaky sea salt

(Continued on page 8)

METHOD

1. **Press the tofu:** Wrap the tofu in paper towels on a plate. Place a heavy object, such as two books or a heavy-bottomed skillet on top of the tofu and press it as you prepare the broth.

2. **Prepare the broth:** Heat 1 teaspoon avocado oil in a wide pot. Add 1 shallot and cook for 2 to 3 minutes until just beginning to soften. Add the mushrooms and cook for 4 to 5 minutes until beginning to brown. Add the garlic, star anise, and white parts of the minced scallions and cook for 45 seconds until fragrant. Pour in the cooking wine, soy sauce, and 1 teaspoon sesame oil and bring to a boil. Stir to coat all of the aromatics.

3. **Simmer the broth:** Add the vegetable stock and bring to a boil. Reduce heat and simmer for 25 minutes, uncovered. Season with salt and pepper to taste. Add the tatsoi to the broth and cover the pot. Cook for 8 to 10 minutes until the leaves and stalks are bright green but tender. Turn off the heat.

4. **Prepare the tofu:** As the tatsoi cooks, cut the pressed tofu into 2-inch cubes. In a bowl, combine the cassava flour with 1 teaspoon salt and ½ teaspoon black pepper. Add the tofu and toss gently to coat.

5. **Fry the tofu:** In a skillet, heat the remaining avocado oil and remaining sesame oil over medium-high heat. Once shimmering, shake any excess flour off the tofu before adding it to the skillet. Cook without moving for 3 to 4 minutes until well-browned. Flip and cook for an additional 2 to 3 minutes until crispy. Transfer to a plate and cover loosely with foil to keep warm. Carefully wipe out the skillet.

6. **Cook the crispy topping:** Heat sesame oil in the same skillet over medium-high heat. Once hot, add remaining shallot and cook for 2 minutes until it begins to soften and brown. Add the peanuts to the skillet and cook 2 minutes more. Turn off the heat and stir in the Thai chili peppers. Allow the residual heat to cook them for 1 minute until fragrant. Transfer the peanuts, shallots, and chili peppers to a bowl. Add the remaining green parts of the minced scallions and sprinkle with flaky sea salt.

7. **To serve:** Ladle the broth into shallow bowls and arrange the braised tatsoi on top. Spoon the peanuts and shallots across the tatsoi and arrange the crispy tofu on top. Enjoy!

Sweet Potato Fritters
with Harissa Sour Cream Sauce

Time to Make: 40 minutes

Serves: 4

WHY THIS RECIPE WORKS

These sweet potato fritters are filled to the brim with flavor. The spicy plant-based sour cream sauce is prepared with a touch of coconut for a subtle hint of rich sweetness. Be sure to refrigerate the remaining canned coconut milk because you will use it in tomorrow's coconut curry soba!

SUBSTITUTIONS

Sweet potatoes: Carrots or zucchini
All-purpose flour: Any flour that suits your dietary needs, such as all-purpose flour, chickpea flour, cassava flour, almond flour, or hazelnut flour
Harissa powder: Create a similar spice blend using the following ingredients: 2 teaspoons chili powder, 1 teaspoon paprika, 1 teaspoon smoked paprika, 1 teaspoon garlic powder, ½ teaspoon cayenne powder, and ½ teaspoon cumin powder
Baby kale: Arugula or baby spinach
Thai chili peppers: Your favorite hot pepper, such as habanero, jalapeño, or serrano

EQUIPMENT & LEFTOVERS

You'll need: Box grater, paper towels, whisk, and skillet
Leftovers: Store the fritters and the sour cream sauce separately in airtight containers in the fridge for 3 days

INGREDIENTS

1 pound sweet potatoes, peeled and grated
½ teaspoon salt plus more to taste
½ cup plant-based sour cream
2 tablespoons coconut milk
1 tablespoon water
2 tablespoons harissa powder, divided
Pepper to taste
5 ounces baby kale
1 teaspoon + 3 tablespoons avocado oil, divided
1 lemon, juiced, divided
4 ounces pomegranate seeds, divided
½ ounce mint, divided
1 Thai chili pepper, thinly sliced
¼ cup liquid egg substitute
⅓ cup all-purpose flour

(Continued on page 11)

METHOD

1. **Prepare the sweet potatoes:** Place the sweet potatoes in a large, paper towel-lined bowl and sprinkle with ½ teaspoon salt. Transfer to the refrigerator for 15 minutes.

2. **While the sweet potatoes are chilling, prepare the sour cream sauce:** Combine the plant-based sour cream with coconut milk, water, and 1 tablespoon harissa powder and whisk to combine. Season with salt and pepper and transfer to the refrigerator.

3. **Prepare the salad:** Combine the baby kale with 1 teaspoon avocado oil and half the lemon juice and massage the leaves gently. Add all but a pinch of the pomegranate seeds. Tear half the mint leaves and add them to the kale salad. Season with salt and pepper. Set aside.

4. **Prepare the mint garnish:** Add the whole mint leaves to a small bowl and add the Thai chili pepper. Add the remaining lemon juice and set aside.

5. **Prepare the sweet potato fritters:** Squeeze out as much liquid as possible from the sweet potatoes and discard the paper towels. Return the sweet potatoes to the bowl. Add the egg substitute, the remaining harissa powder, flour, salt, and pepper and use your hands to mix the ingredients until well-combined. Form the mixture into 8 patties.

6. **Fry the fritters:** Heat the remaining avocado oil in a skillet over medium-high heat. Once the oil is shimmering, add the fritters—in batches, if necessary—and cook until golden brown, about 3 to 4 minutes. Adjust the heat as necessary to keep the fritters from burning. Flip the fritters to the other side and cook for an additional 3 to 4 minutes. Transfer to a plate.

7. **To serve:** Spoon a tablespoon of the harissa sour cream sauce on one side of a rimmed plate and use the back of your spoon to smooth it out. Add two fritters on top of the sauce and scatter the lemony mint leaves and Thai chili peppers on top. Pile the salad next to the fritters and sprinkle with the remaining pomegranate seeds and a dusting of harissa powder, if desired. Enjoy!

Vegan Coconut Curry Soba with Mushrooms

Time to Make: 45 minutes (10 minutes inactive)

Serves: 4

WHY THIS RECIPE WORKS

This soba is rich without being overly decadent. We load up our soba bowls with plenty of shitake, cremini mushrooms, and tender-crisp green beans. The best part? Crispy foraged mushrooms piled on top for a savory, earthy finish. Be sure to use up the rest of the coconut milk you refrigerated from yesterday's recipe.

SUBSTITUTIONS

Shitake and cremini mushrooms: Mix and match your favorite mushroom variety in this dish or try it with eggplant
Green beans: Sugar snap peas, broccoli florets, or baby spinach (cook time may vary)
Soba: Udon or ramen noodles
Maitake mushrooms: More shitake or cremini mushrooms or try it with oyster, king trumpet, or enoki mushrooms

EQUIPMENT & LEFTOVERS

You'll need: Two large pots and a colander
Leftovers: Store the broth and the noodles separately in airtight containers in the fridge for up to 3 days. Drizzle the noodles with a touch of sesame oil to prevent them from sticking.

INGREDIENTS

3 teaspoons avocado oil, divided
1 shallot, peeled and thinly sliced
5 cloves garlic, peeled and minced
3 teaspoons ginger, peeled and freshly minced
4 ounces shitake mushroom caps, thinly sliced
8 ounces cremini mushrooms, thinly sliced
1 tablespoon curry powder
1 teaspoon turmeric, more or less to taste
¾ teaspoon cayenne powder, more or less to taste
Salt and pepper to taste
6 cups vegetable stock
1 (15-ounce) can coconut milk
16 ounces soba noodles
1 teaspoon pure sesame oil
4 ounces maitake or oyster mushrooms, torn into bite-sized pieces
10 ounces fresh green beans, halved
1 lime, cut into wedges
Sesame seeds, optional

(Continued on page 14)

METHOD

1. **Cook the broth aromatics:** Heat 2 teaspoons avocado oil in a large pot over medium heat. Once hot, add the shallot and cook for 3 to 4 minutes until just beginning to soften. Add the garlic and ginger and cook for 1 minute until fragrant.

2. **Sauté the shitake and cremini mushrooms:** Add the shitake and cremini mushrooms to the pot and cook for 5 minutes until they begin to soften. Season with curry powder, turmeric, and cayenne powder and cook for 1 minute until fragrant. Season lightly with salt and pepper.

3. **Simmer the broth:** Add the vegetable stock and bring to a boil. Reduce heat and add the coconut milk. Taste and season lightly with salt and pepper. Simmer for 20 to 25 minutes as you finish the rest of the recipe.

4. **Boil the soba:** Bring a medium pot of water to a boil. Add the soba and cook according to package instructions. Once al dente, drain and rinse. Drizzle with the sesame oil and set aside. Carefully wipe out the pot and return it to the stovetop.

5. **Sauté the maitake or oyster mushrooms:** Heat the remaining avocado oil in the same pot used to boil the soba over medium-high heat. Once hot, add the maitake mushrooms and cook for 3 to 5 minutes per side until crispy and browned all over. Using a slotted spoon, transfer the crispy mushrooms to a bowl and sprinkle with a touch of salt.

6. **Cook the green beans:** While the mushrooms are cooking, turn the heat on the coconut curry broth to medium and add the green beans. Cook for 3 to 5 minutes until tender-crisp. Turn off the heat.

7. **To serve:** Divide the dressed soba noodles between bowls and ladle the coconut curry broth on top. Place the crispy maitake mushrooms on top. Garnish with lime wedges and sesame seeds. Enjoy!

Balsamic Farro Salad with Figs

Time to Make: 40 minutes

Serves: 4

WHY THIS RECIPE WORKS

Balsamic Farro Salad with Figs is sweet, savory, and filling thanks to roasted figs, cherry tomatoes, and an easy balsamic vinaigrette. This recipe is a great way to clear out any leftover herbs or greens. Have a few extra mint leaves or scallions? Chop them up and throw them in right before serving!

SUBSTITUTIONS

Farro: Your favorite rice or grain, such as brown rice, white rice, freekeh, or quinoa (cook time will vary)
Figs: Nectarines, plums, pears, or red seedless grapes

EQUIPMENT & LEFTOVERS

You'll need: Large pot, colander, and baking sheet
Leftovers: Store in an airtight container in the fridge for 3 days

INGREDIENTS

1 cup farro
1 pint figs, halved
1 pint cherry tomatoes, some halved and some left whole
2 tablespoons + ¼ cup extra-virgin olive oil, divided
Salt and pepper to taste
5 ounces baby kale
2 ounces basil leaves, torn
1 tablespoon balsamic vinegar
2 teaspoons maple syrup
1 teaspoon Dijon mustard

METHOD

1. **Preheat oven to 400°F.**

2. **Prepare the farro:** Bring 2 quarts of water to a boil in a large pot. Add the farro and turn the heat to a low boil. Boil for 30 minutes until tender. Drain and rinse briefly.

3. **Roast the figs and tomatoes:** While the farro cooks, arrange the figs (cut-side up) and tomatoes on a baking sheet. Drizzle with 1 tablespoon extra-virgin olive oil and a sprinkle of salt. Transfer to the oven for 15 minutes or until the tomatoes begin to soften and turn golden brown. Turn the broiler on and broil until the tomatoes char and the tops of the figs turn golden brown. Turn off the heat.

4. **Dress the greens:** Combine the baby kale and basil leaves in a large bowl. Drizzle with the 1 tablespoon extra-virgin olive oil and sprinkle with salt and pepper. Toss to coat.

5. **Prepare the balsamic vinaigrette:** In a bowl, whisk together the remaining extra-virgin olive oil, vinegar, maple syrup, and Dijon mustard until emulsified. Season with a sprinkle of salt. Set aside and whisk again before serving.

6. **Prepare the salad:** Transfer the farro to the bowl of greens and toss to combine. Pour the balsamic vinaigrette on top and toss to coat. Add half of the roasted figs and tomatoes and gently toss.

7. **To serve:** Divide the salads between plates and top with the remaining roasted figs and tomatoes. Garnish with a sprinkle of salt. Enjoy!

PLAN 1: WEEK 2

This recipe plan includes dinner recipes for five days, all of which serve four. To conquer the grocery store in one shopping trip, the next page outlines a detailed grocery list, with items separated by store department. You will also find storage, freezing, and thawing tips to help you plan your week. This plan is all about creating a perfect balance between earthy flavors and sweet or rich accompaniments. A creamy beet puree is paired with succulent mushroom medallions while crispy beets are paired with sweet, roasted grapes. Pay special attention to the key players throughout the week (beets and scallions) and be sure to buy the freshest and healthiest of those ingredients that you can find because you will use them for multiple recipes.

THE MENU

MONDAY
Vegan Risotto with Carrot Bolognese

TUESDAY
Seared Mushroom "Scallops" with Beet Puree

WEDNESDAY
Red Lentil Balls with Golden Cauliflower Puree

THURSDAY
Warm Freekeh Salad with Roasted Grapes and Crispy Beets

FRIDAY
Soba with Thai Basil Pesto

PLAN 1: WEEK 2
CONQUERING THE GROCERY STORE

FOOD SAFETY GUIDELINES

Buying groceries for the entire week can require some forethought, so be sure to refer to the FDA's storage and freezing guidelines for your ingredients. To keep herbs and leafy greens fresh through the week, wrap them in a damp paper towel and store in a bag in your crisper. Refresh the paper towel periodically through the week to keep them extra fresh.

GRAINS
- ☐ 1 cup cracked freekeh
- ☐ 1 cup carnaroli rice

OIL
- ☐ Avocado oil

PLANT-BASED DAIRY
- ☐ 1 tablespoon plant-based butter
- ☐ 1 cup store-bought or homemade almond milk ricotta cheese
- ☐ 1 cup plain almond milk Greek yogurt
- ☐ ⅓ cup oat milk

STOCK
- ☐ 7 cups vegetable stock

FRUITS & VEGETABLES
- ☐ 2 yellow onions
- ☐ 1 shallot
- ☐ 1–2 Thai chili peppers
- ☐ 6 cloves garlic
- ☐ 1 pound carrots
- ☐ 8 ounces cremini mushrooms
- ☐ 6 king trumpet mushrooms
- ☐ 2 lemons
- ☐ 2 limes
- ☐ 2 red beets
- ☐ 3 small golden beets
- ☐ 2 Yukon Gold potatoes
- ☐ 1 head cauliflower or 1 (16-ounce) bag pre-cut cauliflower florets
- ☐ 12 ounces sugar snap peas, de-stringed
- ☐ 12 ounces red seedless grapes
- ☐ 1¼ cup fresh parsley
- ☐ 5 scallions
- ☐ 1 cup Thai basil leaves
- ☐ ½ cup cilantro
- ☐ ½ ounce mint leaves
- ☐ 1 avocado

(Continued on next page)

PANTRY & SPICES

- ☐ 1 (28-ounce) can whole peeled tomatoes
- ☐ 16 ounces dry red lentils
- ☐ 16 ounces soba noodles
- ☐ Dried parsley
- ☐ Chili powder
- ☐ Garlic powder
- ☐ Cumin seeds
- ☐ Aleppo pepper flakes, optional
- ☐ 1 cup shelled, unsalted pistachios

- ☐ ⅔ cup panko or breadcrumbs)
- ☐ Vegan mayonnaise
- ☐ Turmeric powder
- ☐ Garlic powder
- ☐ Paprika
- ☐ Sesame oil
- ☐ Flaky sea salt
- ☐ Salt
- ☐ Pepper
- ☐ Crushed red pepper

Vegan Risotto with Carrot Bolognese

Time to Make: 60 minutes (20 minutes inactive)

Serves: 4

WHY THIS RECIPE WORKS

This vegan risotto is prepared with a hearty carrot and mushroom Bolognese and topped with herbed almond milk ricotta. The sweetness of the carrots and earthiness of the mushrooms work fabulously with the moderate acidity of canned tomatoes. Finishing the dish with herbed almond milk ricotta adds the perfect amount of richness to the dish.

SUBSTITUTIONS

Carrots: Golden or red beets
Cremini mushrooms: Use any variety you like, such as shitake, trumpet, or foraged
Carnaroli rice: Arborio rice, farro, or brown rice (cook time will vary)
Plant-based ricotta cheese: Almond milk Greek yogurt or almond milk sour cream

EQUIPMENT & LEFTOVERS

You'll need: Wide pot, medium saucepan, and heat-proof measuring cup
Leftovers: Store in an airtight container in the fridge for 3 days

INGREDIENTS

2 teaspoons avocado oil plus more as needed
1 pound carrots, small-diced
1 yellow onion, peeled and diced
8 ounces cremini mushrooms, small-diced
4 cloves garlic, peeled and minced
Salt, pepper, and crushed red pepper to taste
4–7 cups vegetable stock, divided
1 (28-ounce) can whole peeled tomatoes
1 tablespoon plant-based butter or avocado oil
1 cup carnaroli rice

Herbed Almond Milk Ricotta

1 cup store-bought or homemade almond milk ricotta cheese
¼ cup fresh parsley leaves, minced
¼ teaspoon crushed red pepper
Flaky sea salt to taste
2 teaspoons water, if necessary

(Continued on page 23)

METHOD

1. **Start the carrot Bolognese:** Heat the oil in a wide pot over medium heat. Add the carrots and onion and cook for 4 to 5 minutes until they just begin to soften. Add the mushrooms and cook for 5 to 7 minutes more until the liquid begins to release. Add the garlic and cook for 45 seconds or until fragrant. Season with salt and pepper and crushed red pepper.

2. **Deglaze the pot:** Turn the heat to high. Once the mushrooms begin to crisp up around the edges (about 1 minute), add 1 cup vegetable stock. Scrape up any browned bits stuck to the bottom of the pot and bring to a boil.

3. **Simmer the sauce:** Add the whole peeled tomatoes and bring to a boil. Reduce heat to medium-low. Cover and simmer for 30 minutes until reduced slightly. The carrots should be very, very soft. Taste and season again with salt, pepper, and crushed red pepper.

4. **Prepare the risotto:** Warm the vegetable stock in a heat-proof measuring cup in the microwave. Alternatively, you may simmer the stock in a small saucepan on the stove. Next, heat plant-based butter or avocado oil in a medium saucepan over medium heat. Once it is hot, add the carnaroli rice and toss to coat. Cook for 1 to 2 minutes. Stir the risotto. Ladle in 1 cup of warm vegetable stock. Cook for 2 to 3 minutes until most of the liquid is absorbed. Continue adding stock, alternating stirring and disturbing the rice until the rice is al dente and soft. Be patient! It will take about 30 to 35 minutes total. You may use all the stock or only 3 to 4 cups. Continue stirring until the rice is softened and the sauce is velvety and luxurious. Taste and season with salt and pepper. Turn off the heat and allow the risotto to rest for 5 minutes.

5. **While the rice rests, prepare the herbed almond milk ricotta:** In a bowl, combine the plant-based ricotta, parsley leaves, crushed red pepper, and a touch of flaky sea salt. If the ricotta seems dry, add a splash or two of water and mix with a fork to combine. Set aside.

6. **To serve:** After the risotto has finished resting, add a few spoonsful of the carrot Bolognese to the pot of risotto and toss to combine. Divide the risotto between bowls and pile more sauce on top. Serve with a dollop of the almond milk herbed ricotta and more minced parsley leaves, if desired. Enjoy!

Seared Mushroom "Scallops" with Beet Puree

Time to Make: 45 minutes (20 minutes inactive)

Serves: 4

WHY THIS RECIPE WORKS

Thick rounds of king oyster (also known as king trumpet) mushrooms sear up so beautifully and so quickly in this recipe. Served atop a beautiful puree of beets, this recipe will look and taste like five-star dining. Roast the mushroom caps and use them as your garnish so that no part of the mushroom goes to waste.

SUBSTITUTIONS

Red beets: Golden beets or carrots
King oyster mushrooms: Any variety of mushroom you like

EQUIPMENT & LEFTOVERS

You'll need: Skillet, baking sheet, foil, and food processor
Leftovers: Store in an airtight container in the fridge for 3 days

INGREDIENTS

2 red beets, peeled and diced

2 Yukon Gold potatoes, peeled and diced

1 yellow onion, peeled and quartered

6 tablespoons avocado oil, divided

Salt and pepper to taste

6 king trumpet mushrooms, caps and bodies kept separate

3 tablespoons water plus more as needed

½ cup plain almond milk Greek yogurt

¼ cup fresh parsley, roughly chopped

METHOD

1. **Preheat oven to 425°F.** Line a baking sheet with foil.

2. **Roast the beets:** Arrange the prepared beets, potatoes, and onion on one side of the baking sheet. Drizzle with 2 tablespoons avocado oil and season with salt and pepper. Roast for 25 minutes until almost completely cooked through.

3. **Prepare the mushrooms:** Cut any woody roots off the mushrooms. Cut the caps off the mushrooms, then thinly slice the caps of the mushrooms and set aside. Cut the bodies of the mushrooms into thick rounds and set aside.

4. **Roast the mushroom caps:** Add the mushroom caps to the other side of the baking sheet with the beets and drizzle with 1 tablespoon avocado oil and a sprinkle of salt and pepper. Roast for an additional 10 minutes, flipping the mushrooms once halfway through. Remove the baking sheet from the oven. Transfer the roasted mushroom caps to a bowl.

5. **Prepare the beet puree:** Transfer the beets, potato, and onion to a food processor. Add 2 tablespoons avocado oil, water, and almond milk Greek yogurt to the food processor. Pulse until smooth. Add more water until the puree reaches your desired consistency. Taste and season with salt and pepper. Transfer to a bowl and keep warm.

(Continued on page 26)

6. **Prepare the mushroom caps:** Drizzle the mushroom caps with a touch of avocado oil and toss with the parsley. Set aside.

7. **Sear the mushroom "scallops":** Heat oil in a skillet over medium-high heat until hot. Add the mushroom rounds and cook for 3 to 5 minutes per side until well-seared and tender. Turn off the heat and season them with salt and pepper immediately.

8. **To serve:** Spoon the beet puree onto plates and use the back of your spoon to smooth it. Arrange the sliced mushroom caps and parsley on top and arrange the mushroom "scallops" around the caps. Drizzle with avocado oil, if desired. Enjoy!

Red Lentil Balls with Golden Cauliflower Puree

Time to Make: 45 minutes (10 minutes inactive)

Serves: 4

WHY THIS RECIPE WORKS

These lentil balls are filling, loaded with flavor, and so easy to prepare. We serve these alongside a golden cauliflower puree for a fragrant and aromatic meal.

SUBSTITUTIONS

Red lentils: Brown or green lentils
Shallot: Small yellow onion
Cumin seeds: Cumin powder
Pistachios: Peanuts, walnuts, or cashews
Cauliflower: Peeled potatoes, parsnips, sweet potatoes, or your favorite root vegetable (cook time may vary)

EQUIPMENT & LEFTOVERS

You'll need: Wide pot or skillet, large pot, sieve, and immersion blender (optional)
Leftovers: Store in an airtight container in the fridge for 3 days

INGREDIENTS

16 ounces dry red lentils

1 head cauliflower or 1 (16-ounce) bag pre-cut cauliflower florets

1 shallot, peeled and minced

1 tablespoon dried parsley

2 tablespoons chili powder

2 teaspoons garlic powder

1 teaspoon cumin seeds, lightly crushed between your fingers

1 teaspoon Aleppo pepper flakes, optional

½ teaspoon crushed red pepper plus more to taste

⅔ cup panko or breadcrumbs

2 tablespoons vegan mayonnaise

Salt and pepper to taste

1 tablespoon avocado oil, for frying

½ cup plain almond milk Greek yogurt

⅓ cup oat milk or vegetable stock plus more as needed

2 teaspoons turmeric powder

1 teaspoon garlic powder

1 teaspoon paprika

¼ cup minced parsley

Crushed red pepper, optional

(Continued on page 29)

METHOD

1. **Preheat oven to 200°F.**

2. **Cook the lentils:** Add 5 cups of water to a large pot. Bring to a boil over high heat. Add the lentils and reduce heat to medium. Cook for 8 to 12 minutes until almost completely soft. Drain the lentils into a sieve and rinse under cold water. Wipe out the pot, fill it three-quarters of the way up with water, and return the pot to the stove (you will need it for the next step).

3. **Start the cauliflower puree:** Add the cauliflower florets to the water. Bring to a boil, then reduce heat to medium and cook for 20 to 25 minutes until soft. Drain and return the cauliflower to the pot and set aside.

4. **As you cook the lentils, prepare the spices:** In a large bowl, combine the shallot, parsley, chili powder, garlic powder, cumin seeds, Aleppo pepper flakes (if using), crushed red pepper, panko or breadcrumbs, and vegan mayonnaise. Use a spoon to combine all the ingredients. Season the mixture with salt and pepper.

5. **Form the lentil balls:** Add the lentils to the bowl of spices and use a wooden spoon or your hands to combine the mixture until it is doughy. It shouldn't be too wet or too crumbly. If it seems too wet, add a bit more panko. If it's too dry, add a bit more mayonnaise or a little oil. Taste and season again with salt and pepper. Scoop out a heaping tablespoon of the mixture and roll it into a ball and continue on with the rest of the mixture until all of the lentil balls are formed.

6. **Fry the lentil balls:** Heat avocado oil in a wide pot over medium heat. Add the lentil balls and cook–in batches–for 2 to 3 minutes per side. You want to turn very gently; use the edge of your tongs to release the lentil ball before flipping it. Continue cooking until all the lentil balls are browned and cooked through. Note: You may need to add more oil as you cook them. Add oil in 1 teaspoon increments if the pan becomes too dry. Keep the lentil balls warm in the oven as you fry the rest of the lentil balls.

7. **Finish the cauliflower puree:** Turn the heat on the cauliflower florets to low. Add the almond milk Greek yogurt, oat milk, turmeric, garlic powder, and paprika and stir to combine. Taste and season with salt and pepper. Using an immersion blender, blend until completely pureed and creamy. If you don't have an immersion blender, just use your spoon or a potato masher to completely combine and mash the cauliflower a bit. It will be a bit chunky, but still delicious!

8. **To serve:** Divide the puree between plates and arrange the lentil balls on top. Garnish with more parsley and crushed red pepper, if desired. Enjoy!

Warm Freekeh Salad
with Roasted Grapes and Crispy Beets

Time to Make: 45 minutes (10 minutes inactive)

Serves: 4

WHY THIS RECIPE WORKS

This warm freekeh salad is a divine combination of
complementary flavors and textures. Earthy freekeh
is paired with sweet grapes and tossed with a bright
dressing. We add crunchy pistachios and crisp roasted
golden beets for textural contrast. You can use a
mandoline on the beets, cut them in half and thinly slice
them into half-moons, or small-dice them for an even
quicker meal!

SUBSTITUTIONS

Cracked freekeh: Quinoa or pearl couscous (cook time
may vary)
Golden beets: Red beets or carrots
Red seedless grapes: Black or green seedless grapes,
quartered plums, apple wedges, or roasted cherry
tomatoes
Scallions and parsley: Try it out with basil, mint, or a
few leaves of Thai basil if you have a few to spare from
the Thai Basil Pesto recipe that follows.
Pistachios: Peanuts, walnuts, or cashews

EQUIPMENT & LEFTOVERS

You'll need: Medium pot, colander, paper towels,
baking sheet, and mandoline (optional)
Leftovers: Store in an airtight container in the fridge for
3 days

INGREDIENTS

1 cup cracked freekeh

3 small golden beets, peeled and thinly sliced into
rounds or half-moons

3 teaspoons avocado oil, divided, plus more as needed

Salt and pepper to taste

12 ounces red seedless grapes

2 lemons, juiced

3 scallions, minced

½ cup fresh parsley, finely chopped, plus more for
garnish

½ cup shelled pistachios, lightly crushed, plus more
for garnish

(Continued on page 32)

METHOD

1. **Preheat oven to 400°F.**

2. **Cook the freekeh:** Bring 3 cups of salted water to a boil in a medium pot. Add the cracked freekeh and cook for 20 to 25 minutes until tender. Drain and set aside.

3. **Prepare the crispy golden beets:** Drizzle 1 teaspoon avocado oil on the baking sheet and use a paper towel to coat the bottom of the baking sheet with oil. Add another teaspoon of oil in the center of the baking sheet and add the golden beet slices. Use your hands to coat the beets with oil. Do not add too much oil. Spread the beets on the baking sheet in an even layer, working to ensure that there is no overlap between the beets. Transfer to the oven and roast for 10 minutes until crispy and golden brown. Check on the beets after 7 minutes to ensure that they do not burn. Remove from the oven and transfer to a paper towel-lined plate and immediately sprinkle with salt. Wipe excess oil off the baking sheet.

4. **Roast the grapes:** Drizzle the remaining avocado oil on the baking sheet and add the grapes. Use a spoon to lightly toss the grapes in the oil. Sprinkle with salt and transfer to the oven for 15 to 20 minutes or until the grape skins begin to split and they turn golden brown. Remove from the oven and set aside.

5. **As the grapes roast, prepare the dressing:** In a bowl, combine the lemon juice, scallions, parsley, and pistachios. Season lightly with salt and pepper. Add the warm freekeh and roasted grapes. Season once more with salt and pepper.

6. **To serve:** Divide the dressed freekeh between plates and arrange the crispy beets on top. Garnish with a sprinkle of pistachios and a few parsley leaves. Enjoy!

Soba with Thai Basil Pesto

Time to Make: 30 minutes

Serves: 4

WHY THIS RECIPE WORKS

This recipe is the perfect way to round out your week. Use up any leftover herbs that might be lurking in your crisper. Have a few leftover parsley leaves? Throw them in! It's also unbelievably quick and easy, which means you can jump right into enjoying your weekend.

SUBSTITUTIONS

Soba: Udon, rice noodles, or ramen noodles (cook time will vary)
Sugar snap peas: Edamame or frozen green peas
Thai basil: Italian basil or mint
Thai chili peppers: Crushed red pepper
Pistachios: Peanuts, walnuts, or cashews

EQUIPMENT & LEFTOVERS

You'll need: Large pot, sieve or colander, and food processor
Leftovers: Store in an airtight container in the fridge for 3 days

INGREDIENTS

16 ounces soba noodles

12 ounces sugar snap peas, de-stringed

1 cup loosely packed Thai basil leaves, plus more for garnish

½ cup loosely packed cilantro leaves and tender stems

½ ounce mint leaves

2 scallions

1–2 Thai chili peppers, stems removed

2 cloves garlic, peeled

2 teaspoons pure sesame oil

1 lime, juiced

¼ cup shelled pistachios

Salt and pepper to taste

1 avocado

1 lime, cut into 6 wedges

(Continued on page 35)

METHOD

1. **Cook the soba:** Bring a large pot of salted water to a boil. Add the soba and cook for 6 minutes until just shy of al dente. Add the sugar snap peas to the boiling water and cook for 2 minutes until the soba is al dente and the sugar snap peas are bright green and tender-crisp. Drain through a sieve and rinse with cold water. Set aside.

2. **While you wait for the water to boil, prepare the Thai basil pesto:** In a food processor, combine the Thai basil leaves, cilantro leaves and tender stems, mint leaves, scallions, Thai chili peppers, garlic cloves, sesame oil, lime juice, and pistachios. Pulse until pureed to your desired consistency. Taste and season with salt and pepper.

3. **Prepare the avocado:** Peel the avocado and cut in half around the pit. Remove and discard the pit. Thinly slice each half and squeeze juice from 2 lime wedges over the avocado. Sprinkle it with salt and set aside.

4. **To serve:** Pour the Thai basil pesto into a large bowl. Add the drained soba noodles and sugar snap peas to the bowl and toss until completely coated. Divide the coated soba noodles between bowls. Arrange the sliced avocado on each bowl and garnish with a lime wedge and a few additional Thai basil leaves. Enjoy!

PLAN 1: WEEK 3

This recipe plan includes dinner recipes for five days, all of which serve four. To conquer the grocery store in one shopping trip, the next page outlines a detailed grocery list, with items separated by store department. You will also find storage, freezing, and thawing tips to help you plan your week. This plan is all about big, contrasting flavors like lentil salad dressed with a sweet and spicy maple vinaigrette. Pay special attention to the key players throughout the week (mushrooms, cilantro, and curly kale) and be sure to buy the freshest and healthiest of those ingredients that you can find because you will use them for multiple recipes.

THE MENU

MONDAY
Vegan Burrito Bowl with Stewed Mushrooms

TUESDAY
Harissa-Maple Lentil Salad

WEDNESDAY
Quinoa-Stuffed Poblano Peppers

THURSDAY
Aji Amarillo Risotto with Crispy Kale

FRIDAY
Sesame-Soy Braised Mushrooms with Coconut Milk Grits

PLAN 1: WEEK 3
CONQUERING THE GROCERY STORE

FOOD SAFETY GUIDELINES

Buying groceries for the entire week can require some forethought, so be sure to refer to the FDA's storage and freezing guidelines for your ingredients. To keep herbs and leafy greens fresh through the week, wrap them in a damp paper towel and store in a bag in your crisper. Refresh the paper towel periodically through the week to keep them extra fresh.

GRAINS
- ☐ 1 cup uncooked wild rice
- ☐ 1 cup quinoa
- ☐ 1 cup uncooked carnaroli or arborio rice

OIL
- ☐ Avocado oil
- ☐ Extra-virgin olive oil

PLANT-BASED DAIRY
- ☐ ½ cup plain almond milk Greek yogurt

STOCK
- ☐ 8¼ cups vegetable stock

FRUITS & VEGETABLES
- ☐ 2 yellow onions
- ☐ 3 shallots
- ☐ 1 leek
- ☐ 2 carrots
- ☐ 1 pound (1 whole) acorn squash
- ☐ 1 pound (2 whole) sweet potatoes
- ☐ 2 pounds + 8 ounces cremini mushrooms
- ☐ 1 pound mixed mushrooms, such as cremini, shitake, oyster, beech, or maitake
- ☐ 5 poblano peppers
- ☐ 10 ounces chopped curly kale
- ☐ 8 ounces fresh or frozen green peas
- ☐ 2 Roma tomatoes
- ☐ 2 lemons
- ☐ 4 limes
- ☐ 8 scallions
- ☐ 1½ cups parsley
- ☐ ¾ cup cilantro
- ☐ 1 avocado

PANTRY & SPICES
- ☐ 1 (15-ounce) can black beans
- ☐ 1 (15-ounce) can coconut milk
- ☐ 16 ounces French green lentils
- ☐ 1 cup polenta corn grits
- ☐ Cassava or all-purpose flour
- ☐ Maple syrup
- ☐ Vegan mayonnaise
- ☐ Ají amarillo paste
- ☐ Chili powder
- ☐ Paprika
- ☐ Cumin powder
- ☐ Garlic powder
- ☐ Ground cinnamon
- ☐ Cayenne powder
- ☐ Harissa powder
- ☐ Soy sauce
- ☐ Sesame oil
- ☐ Shichimi-togarashi, optional
- ☐ Salt
- ☐ Pepper
- ☐ Cassava tortillas, optional

Vegan Burrito Bowl with Stewed Mushrooms

Time to Make: 55 minutes (15 minutes inactive)

Serves: 4

WHY THIS RECIPE WORKS

Mushrooms are so earthy and meaty on their own in this recipe, but I stretch them a bit further by adding a can of black beans. I prefer to mince most of the mushrooms and chop a few into quarters for a little textural variety, but you may opt to mince all of the mushrooms to save yourself an additional step.

SUBSTITUTIONS

Wild rice: Quinoa, white rice, freekeh, or lentils (cook time will vary)
Cremini mushrooms: Any fresh mushroom variety

EQUIPMENT & LEFTOVERS

You'll need: Small pot with lid, food processor, and wide pot
Leftovers: Store in an airtight container in the fridge for 3 days

INGREDIENTS

1 cup uncooked wild rice

1¾ cups water

Salt and pepper to taste

2 pounds cremini mushrooms, divided

2 teaspoons avocado oil

1 yellow onion, peeled and diced

1 tablespoon cumin powder

1 tablespoon chili powder

2 teaspoons paprika

1 teaspoon garlic powder

¼ teaspoon ground cinnamon

Cayenne powder to taste

1 (15-ounce) can black beans, drained

½ cup plain almond milk Greek yogurt

½ cup cilantro leaves and tender stems, minced, plus more for garnish

2 limes, divided

3 scallions, minced, divided

1 avocado, for serving

Cassava tortillas, optional, for serving

(Continued on next page)

METHOD

1. **Cook the rice:** Combine the wild rice, water, and a sprinkle of salt to a small pot. Bring to a boil, stir once, then reduce heat and cover. Simmer for 45 minutes. Turn off the heat and allow the rice to rest for 10 minutes before removing the lid and fluffing with a fork.

2. **Prepare the mushrooms:** Add 1½ pounds mushrooms to a food processor and pulse until finely chopped. Quarter or halve the remaining ½ pound mushrooms.

3. **Cook the onion:** Heat the avocado oil in a wide pot over medium heat. Once hot, add the onion and cook for 4 to 5 minutes until it just begins to turn golden around the edges.

4. **Cook the mushrooms:** Add the ½ pound of quartered/halved mushrooms to the pot and cook, stirring occasionally, for 8 to 9 minutes until they release liquid and begin to turn golden brown. Season with salt and pepper, then add the minced mushrooms to the pot. Cook for 10 to 15 minutes, turning occasionally, until all the liquid releases and evaporates. Season with salt and pepper. Season the mushrooms with cumin powder, chili powder, paprika, garlic powder, cinnamon, cayenne, and salt and pepper to taste.

5. **Add the black beans to mushrooms:** Reduce heat and simmer, uncovered, for 20 minutes. If the mushrooms stick, throw in a splash of water to loosen them up.

6. **Prepare the cilantro crema:** Meanwhile, combine the almond milk yogurt, cilantro, and juice from 1 lime in a bowl and stir until combined. Season with salt and transfer to the refrigerator until needed.

7. **Finish the mushrooms:** Stir the white parts of the scallions into the stewed mushrooms and cook for 2 minutes. Turn off the heat.

8. **Right before serving:** Peel the avocado and remove and discard the pit. Dice the avocado. Cut the remaining lime into wedges.

9. **To serve:** Divide the wild rice between plates or shallow bowls. If desired, serve with charred or steamed cassava flour tortillas. Pile the stewed mushrooms on top and spoon the avocado on top of each dish. Garnish with remaining scallion greens, a pinch of cilantro, and lime wedges. Drizzle each dish with the cilantro crema. Enjoy!

Harissa-Maple Lentil Salad

Time to Make: 30 minutes

Serves: 4

WHY THIS RECIPE WORKS

Big, bold flavors and only thirty minutes? This recipe really is a dream. Harissa-Maple Lentil Salad combines the sweet, smoky, spicy flavors of harissa and maple with perfectly roasted, slightly charred tomatoes and carrots. Finished with bright scallions, parsley, and a little lemon juice, it's a flavor trifecta.

SUBSTITUTIONS

French green lentils: Black lentils, freekeh, or quinoa (cook time will vary)
Carrots: Golden beets or sweet potatoes
Roma tomatoes: Cherry or grape tomatoes, halved
Harissa powder: Create a similar spice blend using the following ingredients: 1 teaspoon chili powder, ½ teaspoon paprika, ½ teaspoon smoked paprika, ½ teaspoon garlic powder, ¼ teaspoon cayenne powder, and ¼ teaspoon cumin powder
Maple syrup: Agave syrup or brown sugar dissolved in warm water

EQUIPMENT & LEFTOVERS

You'll need: Medium pot, fine mesh sieve, and baking sheet
Leftovers: Store in an airtight container in the fridge for 3 days

INGREDIENTS

16 ounces French green lentils

2 carrots, peeled and sliced on a bias about ¼-inch thick

1 tablespoon avocado oil, for roasting

Salt and pepper to taste

½ cup extra-virgin olive oil

1 tablespoon harissa powder

½ teaspoon cayenne powder, optional

1 lemon, juiced

2 tablespoons maple syrup

2 Roma tomatoes, cut into wedges

1 large shallot, peeled and sliced into thin wedges

3 scallions, minced

1 cup loosely packed parsley leaves

(Continued on page 43)

METHOD

1. **Preheat oven to 425°F.**

2. **Cook the lentils:** Bring a medium pot of unsalted water to a boil. Add the lentils and cook until al dente, about 15 to 20 minutes. Do not salt them while they cook and do not overcook them. Drain and rinse.

3. **Roast the carrots:** Meanwhile, lay the carrot slices on a baking sheet in an even layer and drizzle with avocado oil. Season with salt and pepper. Roast for 10 minutes until they just begin to soften and brown.

4. **Prepare the dressing:** As the carrots roast, in a bowl combine the extra-virgin olive oil, harissa powder, cayenne powder, lemon juice, maple syrup, and salt and pepper to taste and whisk until well-combined. Taste and season to your preferences.

5. **Prepare the tomatoes:** Combine the tomatoes and shallot in a small bowl and toss with 2 tablespoons of the dressing. Sprinkle lightly with salt. Set aside.

6. **Roast the tomatoes:** Pour the dressed tomatoes on the same baking sheet with the carrots and cook for 10 minutes more. If desired, broil for 2 to 3 minutes until the tops of the tomatoes char. Turn off the heat.

7. **Finish the salad:** Transfer the drained lentils to a bowl and season with salt and pepper. Add the scallions and parsley and toss to combine. Pour 3 tablespoons of the dressing on the salad and toss to coat. Set aside.

8. **To serve:** Divide the dressed lentils between bowls. Pile the roasted carrots and tomatoes on top. Serve with more dressing. Enjoy!

Quinoa-Stuffed Poblano Peppers

Time to Make: 60 minutes (15 minutes inactive)

Serves: 4

WHY THIS RECIPE WORKS

These stuffed poblano peppers are bursting with flavor, literally! We overstuffed them and broiled the tops to crisp up the quinoa on top for a bit of an additional crunch. You'll be spending the most time prepping your poblano peppers, but don't fret if you can't get every single piece of skin off the pepper. Poblanos are typically mild, though some can carry a bit of extra heat. If you're worried about the heat, you can replace them with sweet red bell peppers and stuff them from the top as opposed to splitting them down the side. Don't feel like fussing with stuffing them? Simply chop up all the roasted peppers and throw them in with your quinoa mixture and cook on medium heat for 5 minutes. Serve as a veggie bowl, drizzled with the dressing.

SUBSTITUTIONS

Poblano peppers: Red bell peppers
Quinoa: Freekeh or white rice (cook time will vary)
Cremini mushrooms: Shitake mushrooms
Sweet potatoes: Carrots or golden beets

EQUIPMENT & LEFTOVERS

You'll need: Fine mesh sieve, small pot, baking sheet, plastic wrap or clean towel, and wide pot
Leftovers: Store in an airtight container in the fridge for 3 days

INGREDIENTS

1 cup quinoa

1 teaspoon + 3 tablespoons avocado oil, divided

Salt and pepper to taste

5 poblano peppers

1 yellow onion, peeled and diced

8 ounces cremini mushrooms, diced

1 pound (2 whole) sweet potatoes, peeled and diced

1 tablespoon chili powder

1 tablespoon cumin powder

2 teaspoons garlic powder

2 teaspoons paprika

½ teaspoon cayenne powder, optional

¼ cup vegetable stock or water

⅓ cup vegan mayonnaise

2 limes, juiced

¼ cup loosely packed parsley leaves and tender stems, minced

¼ cup loosely packed cilantro leaves and tender stems, minced

(Continued on next page)

METHOD

1. **Preheat oven to 425°F.**

2. **Cook the quinoa:** Rinse the quinoa under cold water in a fine mesh sieve for 1 minute. In a small pot, heat 1 teaspoon avocado oil over medium heat until hot. Add the quinoa and cook, stirring, for 2 to 3 minutes until it begins to toast and turn golden brown. Pour in 2 cups of water and ¼ teaspoon salt and bring to a boil. Reduce heat to a simmer and cook for 15 to 20 minutes or until the quinoa absorbs all the water. Turn off the heat and set aside.

3. **Roast the poblano peppers:** Drizzle the poblano peppers with 2 tablespoons avocado oil and toss to coat with the oil. Transfer to the oven and roast for 8 minutes per side. Continue to flip periodically until the peppers are charred and blistered.

4. **Rest the peppers:** Transfer the poblano peppers to a heat-proof bowl and cover with plastic wrap or a clean towel. Let stand for 15 minutes. This will steam the peppers and make them easier to peel. Leave the oven set to 425°F.

5. **Prepare the quinoa stuffing:** Heat the remaining avocado oil in a wide pot over medium-high heat. Add the onion and mushrooms and cook for 7 to 8 minutes until they begin to soften. Season with salt and pepper. Next, add the diced sweet potatoes and cook, stirring occasionally, for 15 minutes until they begin to char and soften. Season lightly with salt and pepper.

6. **Once the sweet potatoes are mostly fork tender, bloom the spices:** Add the chili powder, cumin powder, garlic powder, paprika, and cayenne powder and cook for 1 minute until fragrant. Add the stock or water and scrape up anything stuck to the bottom of the pot. Taste and season to your preferences. Turn the heat to low.

7. **Finish the quinoa stuffing:** Add the cooked quinoa to the pot of stuffing and toss to combine. Cook for 1 to 2 minutes more and turn off the heat.

8. **Peel the peppers:** Peel the peppers, being careful not to break them. Carefully cut a slit down the middle of each pepper and scoop out the seeds. Tip the pepper over and shake out any excess oil or water from inside the pepper. As you peel and deseed each pepper, transfer four of them to the same baking sheet you used before.

9. **Prep the last pepper:** For your last pepper, cut off the top and roughly chop the body. Add it to the pot of quinoa stuffing.

10. **Stuff and bake the peppers:** Using a spoon, carefully stuff each pepper with the quinoa stuffing. Bake them for 5 minutes. Turn on the broiler and broil for 3 minutes to crisp up the top of the quinoa. Turn off the heat and remove from the oven. Note: If you do not use all the stuffing, you can serve the peppers with additional quinoa on the side.

11. **While the peppers bake, prepare the dressing:** In a bowl, combine the vegan mayonnaise, lime juice, cilantro, and parsley. Add ¼ cup water to thin out the dressing and season with salt. Set aside.

12. **To serve:** Use a spatula to transfer the stuffed poblano peppers to plates. Drizzle with the creamy herb dressing and more stuffing on the side. Enjoy!

Ají Amarillo Risotto with Crispy Kale

Time to Make: 30 minutes

Serves: 4

WHY THIS RECIPE WORKS

Ají amarillo paste is a beautiful yellow pepper paste originating from Peru. In Peru, it is often prepared from scratch nearly daily, but there are store-bought varieties available to those who do not have access to the ají amarillo pepper. Depending on the brand, it can vary significantly in heat but is, in general, quite spicy. If you can't find ají amarillo paste, you can use a red pepper paste of your choosing or simply omit it and add a dash of crushed red pepper to the shallots as you sauté them.

SUBSTITUTIONS

Shallots: Small yellow onion
Ají amarillo paste: Red pepper paste of your choosing or crushed red pepper
Green peas: Edamame or chopped sugar snap peas

EQUIPMENT & LEFTOVERS

You'll need: Baking sheet, medium pot, glass measuring cup, and Microplane
Leftovers: Store in an airtight container in the fridge for 3 days

INGREDIENTS

5 ounces chopped curly kale leaves

2 tablespoons avocado oil, divided

Salt and pepper to taste

2 shallots, peeled and minced

1–2 tablespoons ají amarillo paste

4–6 cups vegetable stock, warmed up

1 cup carnaroli or arborio rice

8 ounces fresh or frozen green peas

¼ cup fresh parsley leaves, minced

1 lemon, juiced and zested

METHOD

1. **Preheat oven to 300°F.**

2. **Cook the kale chips:** Arrange the kale leaves on a baking sheet in an even layer. Drizzle with 1 tablespoon avocado oil and use your hands to massage the oil into the leaves. Sprinkle them with salt. Transfer to the oven for 10 to 15 minutes or until the leaves are crispy. Turn off the heat and leave the chips in the oven as you finish the rest of the recipe.

3. **Prepare the ají amarillo paste:** Heat the remaining avocado oil in a medium pot. Add the shallots and cook for 1 to 3 minutes until just beginning to soften. Add the ají amarillo paste and cook for 1 minute until fragrant.

4. **Cook the risotto:** Add the carnaroli rice and cook for 2 minutes until the rice is coated with the paste and begins to toast slightly. Reduce heat to low. Add a ladle of the vegetable stock and stir continuously until the rice absorbs the broth. Continue on, alternating adding stock and stirring, until the liquid is almost completely absorbed. You may only need 3 cups of stock or you may need all 6. Just continue stirring the risotto and adding stock until the rice is tender. Be patient! It may take 30 to 35 minutes.

(Continued on page 49)

5. **Cook the peas:** Stir the peas into the risotto and cook for 2 to 3 minutes until any remaining liquid is absorbed and the peas are bright green. Taste and season with salt and pepper. Turn off the heat and rest the risotto for 5 minutes.

6. **Prepare the garnish:** In a small bowl, combine the parsley, lemon juice and zest, and a pinch of salt and stir to combine. Set aside.

7. **To serve:** Divide the warm risotto between shallow bowls. Add a teaspoon of the parsley mixture on top and garnish with the crispy kale chips. Enjoy!

Sesame-Soy Braised Mushrooms with Coconut Milk Grits

Time to Make: 30 minutes

Serves: 4

WHY THIS RECIPE WORKS

Savory grits take on a subtly sweet flavor when using a can of coconut milk as the cooking liquid. Paired with beautifully braised mushrooms and roasted squash, this recipe takes simple ingredients and transforms them into an unforgettable meal.

SUBSTITUTIONS

Acorn squash: Butternut squash or sweet potatoes (cooking time may vary)
Leek: Yellow onion
Curly kale: Baby spinach

EQUIPMENT & LEFTOVERS

You'll need: Baking sheet, wide pot, medium pot, and whisk
Leftovers: Store in an airtight container in the fridge for 3 days

INGREDIENTS

1 pound (1 whole) acorn squash

2 tablespoons avocado oil, divided

Salt and pepper to taste

1 leek, thinly sliced

1 pound mixed mushrooms, such as cremini, shitake, oyster, beech, or maitake

2 teaspoons soy sauce

2 teaspoons pure sesame oil

2 tablespoons cassava or all-purpose flour

2 cups vegetable stock plus more as needed

1 (15-ounce) can coconut milk

1 cup water

1 cup polenta corn grits

5 ounces chopped curly kale

2 scallions, minced, for garnish

A few shakes of shichimi-togarashi, optional

(Continued on next page)

METHOD

1. **Preheat oven to 400°F.**

2. **Prepare the acorn squash:** Cut the ends off the acorn squash and cut the squash in half lengthwise. Scoop out the seeds and discard them. Flip the acorn squash so it is cut-side down and slice into ½-inch thick half-moons. Transfer to a baking sheet and brush with 1 tablespoon avocado oil. Season with salt and pepper. Transfer to the oven for 15 minutes. Flip and cook for an additional 10 to 15 minutes until the squash is browned and very soft. Turn off the oven and leave the squash in the oven as you finish the rest of the recipe.

3. **Prepare the braised mushrooms:** Heat the remaining avocado oil in a wide pot over medium heat. Add the leek and cook, stirring occasionally, for 6 to 7 minutes until it just begins to soften. Add the mixed mushrooms to the pot and use your spoon to arrange them in a mostly even layer. Cook, without disturbing too often, for 8 to 10 minutes, adjusting the heat as necessary to prevent them from burning. Once the mushrooms are very golden brown, season lightly with salt and pepper. Add the soy sauce and sesame oil and toss to coat.

4. **Simmer the mushrooms:** Sprinkle the mushrooms and leeks with flour and toss to coat. Allow the flour and mushrooms to sizzle in the pan for 1 to 2 minutes. Pour in 1 cup vegetable stock and whisk to incorporate it into the flour mixture. Pour in the remaining stock and continue whisking until smooth. Bring to a boil, then reduce heat and simmer for 15 to 20 minutes. If the sauce seems too thick or reduces too quickly, add a bit more vegetable stock in ¼ cup increments, whisking to incorporate it.

5. **As the mushrooms simmer, prepare the grits:** Pour the coconut milk and water into a medium pot and season with ½ teaspoon salt. Bring to a low boil and add the corn grits. Once the mixture begins to bubble again, reduce heat to low and whisk constantly until thickened and tender, about 15 to 20 minutes. Taste and season with salt and pepper.

6. **Cook the kale:** After the mushrooms have simmered, stir the chopped kale leaves into the broth and cook for 5 minutes until wilted and tender. Season one final time with salt and pepper. Turn off the heat.

7. **To serve:** Divide the coconut milk grits between shallow bowls and pile the sesame-soy braised mushrooms on top. Place a few slices of acorn squash on each dish. Garnish with minced scallions and shichimi-togarashi, if desired. Enjoy!

PLAN 1: WEEK 4

This recipe plan includes dinner recipes for five days, all of which serve four. To conquer the grocery store in one shopping trip, the next page outlines a detailed grocery list, with items separated by store department. You will also find storage, freezing, and thawing tips to help you plan your week. This plan focuses on bright garnishes to complete your meals. Pay special attention to the key players throughout the week (scallions and jalapeño peppers) and be sure to buy the freshest and healthiest of those ingredients that you can find because you will use them for multiple recipes.

THE MENU

MONDAY
Curry Glass Noodle Soup with
Acorn Squash

TUESDAY
Spicy Stewed Black Beans with Crispy
Plantains

WEDNESDAY
Quinoa-Carrot Fritters with Turmeric
Yogurt

THURSDAY
Black Pepper Tofu in Miso Sesame
Broth

FRIDAY
Shredded Mushroom Tacos

PLAN 1: WEEK 4
CONQUERING THE GROCERY STORE

FOOD SAFETY GUIDELINES

Buying groceries for the entire week can require some forethought, so be sure to refer to the FDA's storage and freezing guidelines for your ingredients. To keep herbs and leafy greens fresh through the week, wrap them in a damp paper towel and store in a bag in your crisper. Refresh the paper towel periodically through the week to keep them extra fresh.

PLANT-BASED PROTEIN

- ☐ ¼ cup liquid egg substitute
- ☐ 1 pound extra-firm tofu

GRAINS

- ☐ 16 ounces quinoa
- ☐ 1 cup uncooked white rice

OIL

- ☐ Avocado oil

PLANT-BASED DAIRY

- ☐ ¾ cup plain cashew milk or plain almond milk
  Greek yogurt

STOCK

- ☐ 13 cups vegetable stock

FRUITS & VEGETABLES

- ☐ 3 yellow onions
- ☐ 2 shallots
- ☐ 2 red onions
- ☐ 1 bulb garlic
- ☐ 6 king trumpet mushrooms
- ☐ 8 ounces shitake mushrooms
- ☐ 1 acorn squash
- ☐ 5 carrots
- ☐ 5 ounces baby spinach
- ☐ 8 ounces fresh green beans
- ☐ 10 ounces Brussels sprouts
- ☐ 1 small head savoy cabbage
- ☐ 2 jalapeño peppers
- ☐ 1 red Fresno chili pepper
- ☐ 1 yellow plantain
- ☐ 1 pint cherry tomatoes
- ☐ 5 limes
- ☐ 2 lemons
- ☐ 12 scallions
- ☐ 1 cup cilantro
- ☐ 1 avocado

PANTRY & SPICES

- ☐ 3 (15-ounce) cans black beans, drained
- ☐ 1 (15-ounce) can diced tomatoes
- ☐ 1 (7-ounce) can hot green chili peppers
- ☐ 9 ounces glass noodles (also known as cellophane or bean thread noodles)
- ☐ ¾ cup panko or breadcrumbs
- ☐ 1 cup unsalted peanuts
- ☐ White miso paste
- ☐ Tahini
- ☐ Vegan mayonnaise
- ☐ Maple syrup
- ☐ Pure cane sugar (or use maple syrup), optional
- ☐ 12 small corn tortilla shells
- ☐ Cassava flour
- ☐ Madras curry powder
- ☐ Turmeric powder
- ☐ Garam masala
- ☐ Curry powder
- ☐ Chili powder
- ☐ Cayenne powder
- ☐ Cumin powder
- ☐ Sesame oil
- ☐ Soy sauce
- ☐ Sesame seeds
- ☐ Flaky sea salt
- ☐ Salt
- ☐ Pepper
- ☐ Crushed red pepper

Curry Glass Noodle Soup with Acorn Squash

Time to Make: 40 minutes

Serves: 4

WHY THIS RECIPE WORKS

The rich, aromatic curry broth that's big on flavor and heat is the star of the show in this recipe. Topped with a bright garnish of scallions, lime juice, and onions, this dish is full of wonderfully contrasting yet complementary ingredients.

SUBSTITUTIONS

Madras curry powder: Your favorite curry powder plus additional cayenne or crushed red pepper.
Acorn squash: Butternut squash or 2 large sweet potatoes
Green greens: Edamame or green peas
Glass noodles: Vermicelli, soba, or udon (cook time will vary)

EQUIPMENT & LEFTOVERS

You'll need: 2 large pots, colander
Leftovers: Store in an airtight container in the fridge for 3 days

INGREDIENTS

2 teaspoons avocado oil

1 yellow onion, peeled and thinly sliced into half moons

1 tablespoon Madras curry powder

1 teaspoon turmeric powder

½ teaspoon crushed red pepper to taste

6 cups vegetable stock

Salt and pepper to taste

1 acorn squash, seeded

9 ounces glass noodles (also known as cellophane or bean thread noodles)

3 scallions, minced

1 small red onion, very thinly sliced

1 lime, juiced

8 ounces fresh green beans

METHOD

1. **Start the broth:** Heat the avocado oil in a large pot over medium heat. Add the yellow onion and cook, stirring occasionally, for 5 to 7 minutes until it just begins to soften. Sprinkle the onions with the Madras curry powder, turmeric powder, and crushed red pepper. Cook for 1 minute until aromatic. Pour in the vegetable stock and bring to a boil. Taste and season with salt and pepper. Reduce heat to a simmer.

2. **Prepare the acorn squash:** Cut each half of the seeded squash crosswise into 1-inch wide half-moons. Cut each slice in half to create a quarter moon slice.

3. **Simmer the acorn squash:** Transfer the acorn squash to the simmering liquid and cook, uncovered, over low heat for 20 minutes until fork tender.

4. **Cook the noodles:** Meanwhile, bring a large pot of water to a boil. Add the noodles and cook for 2 to 3 minutes until tender. Drain and rinse with cold water. Note: You may need to refresh the noodles with cold water right before serving.

5. **Prepare the scallion garnish:** In a small bowl, combine the scallions, red onion, and lime juice. Season with salt and transfer to the refrigerator.

6. **Cook the green beans:** Add the green beans to the broth and cook for 5 minutes until bright green and tender-crisp. Turn off the heat.

7. **To serve:** Divide the cooked noodles between bowls and ladle the broth on top. Pile the acorn squash and green beans on top. Divide the scallion garnish between each bowl. Enjoy!

Spicy Stewed Black Beans with Crispy Plantains

Time to Make: 1 hour 10 minutes (30 minutes inactive)

Serves: 4

WHY THIS RECIPE WORKS

Black beans are amped up with curry powder, chili powder, and an extra dose of heat from a jalapeño (or habanero, if you're feeling dangerous!). This recipe comes together in a flash, but the flavor and textural contrast in the final dish doesn't taste rushed at all.

SUBSTITUTIONS

Carrots: Sweet potatoes
Black beans: Pinto beans
Plantain: Any vegetable amenable to thinly slicing and baking into chips, such as a golden beet, carrot, or sweet potato

EQUIPMENT & LEFTOVERS

You'll need: Large pot, baking sheet, mandoline, and paper towels
Leftovers: Store spicy stewed black beans in an airtight container in the fridge for 3 days and store plantain chips in an airtight bag

INGREDIENTS

5 teaspoons avocado oil, divided, plus more as needed

1 yellow onion, peeled and diced

2 carrots, peeled and diced

Salt and pepper to taste

4 cloves garlic, peeled and minced

3 scallions, minced, divided

1 jalapeño, minced (seeds removed, if desired)

1 tablespoon curry powder

1 tablespoon chili powder

1 tablespoon pure cane sugar or maple syrup, optional

1 cup vegetable stock

2 (15-ounce) cans black beans, drained

1 (15-ounce) can diced tomatoes

1 yellow plantain

1 pint cherry tomatoes

1 avocado

2 limes, divided

(Continued on page 60)

METHOD

1. **Preheat oven to 375°F.**

2. **Prepare the stewed black beans:** Heat 2 teaspoons avocado oil in a large heavy-bottomed pot. Once hot, add the onion and carrots and cook for 8 to 10 minutes until softened. Season with salt and pepper. Add garlic, scallion whites, and jalapeño and cook for 30 seconds. Add the curry powder, chili powder, and sugar or syrup and cook for 1 minute until fragrant. Adjust the heat as necessary to prevent the garlic from burning. Pour in the vegetable stock and scrape up anything stuck to the bottom of the pot. Add the black beans and diced tomatoes and bring to a boil. Reduce heat and simmer, uncovered, for 30 to 40 minutes until the beans are very tender. Use your spoon to mash some of the beans against the side of the pot to thicken the stewed beans even further. If the beans thicken up too much, add a splash of water or stock to loosen them up.

3. **Prepare the crispy plantains:** Use a sharp knife to make a cut down the side of the plantain to remove the peel. Cut the ends off. Use a mandoline or a very sharp knife to thinly slice the plantain into paper-thin rounds. Drizzle 1 teaspoon avocado oil on a baking sheet and use your hands to spread it around the bottom of the pan. Arrange the plantain slices in an even layer on the pan and drizzle with the remaining oil. Use your hands or a brush to gently toss the plantains in the oil, then return them to an even layer.

4. **Bake the plantain chips:** Transfer the baking sheet to the oven and bake for 20 minutes until crispy and golden brown. Remove from the oven and transfer to a paper towel-lined plate. Sprinkle them with salt.

5. **Blister the cherry tomatoes:** Turn the oven up to 450°F. Arrange the cherry tomatoes on the same baking sheet. If necessary, add another drizzle of oil. Sprinkle them with salt. Transfer to the oven for 10 minutes until blistered. If desired, broil for 2 to 3 minutes at the end to char them. Remove from the oven and set aside.

6. **Prepare the avocado garnish:** Peel the avocado and cut in half lengthwise. Discard the pit. Dice the avocado and transfer to a bowl with the juice from 1 lime. Add the blistered cherry tomatoes and toss gently to combine. Season with salt and set aside.

7. **To serve:** Divide the black beans between shallow bowls. Spoon the avocado and blistered cherry tomatoes on top. Garnish with crispy plantains, minced scallion greens, and lime wedges. Enjoy!

Quinoa-Carrot Fritters with Turmeric Yogurt

Time to Make: 50 minutes

Serves: 4

WHY THIS RECIPE WORKS

These fritters are crispy on the outside but so pillowy and soft on the inside. Garam masala adds an earthy sweetness to the fritters while the bitter creaminess of the turmeric yogurt takes this dish over the top.

SUBSTITUTIONS

Quinoa: Red lentils (cooking time will vary)
Carrots: Sweet potatoes
Red Fresno chili pepper: Your favorite hot pepper, such as habanero, jalapeño, or serrano, or crushed red pepper to taste

EQUIPMENT & LEFTOVERS

You'll need: Medium pot, box grater, food processor, whisk, skillet, and paper towels
Leftovers: Store in an airtight container in the fridge for 3 days

INGREDIENTS

16 ounces quinoa

½ cup loosely packed cilantro leaves, plus more for garnish

2 shallots, divided

3 cloves garlic, peeled

3 carrots, grated

1 tablespoon garam masala

½ teaspoon cayenne powder

¾ cup panko or breadcrumbs

¼ cup liquid egg substitute

¾ cup plain cashew milk yogurt or plain almond milk Greek yogurt

4–5 tablespoons water, divided, plus more as needed

2 lemons, juiced

2 teaspoons turmeric powder

Salt and pepper to taste

1 tablespoon maple syrup

1 small head savoy cabbage, thinly sliced

1 red Fresno chili pepper, thinly sliced into rounds

1 tablespoon avocado oil, for frying

Flaky sea salt

(Continued on page 63)

METHOD

1. **Cook the quinoa:** Fill a medium pot with water and add the quinoa. Bring to a boil, reduce heat, and simmer for 15 to 20 minutes until tender. Drain and rinse with cold water.

2. **Meanwhile, prepare the fritters:** Combine the cilantro, 1 shallot, and garlic cloves in a food processor and pulse until finely minced. Transfer to a large bowl, then add the carrots, garam masala, cayenne powder, panko or breadcrumbs, egg substitute, and cooked quinoa. Use your hands to firmly combine the ingredients. The more you squash and squeeze the quinoa together, the more the fritters will stay together when fried. To test whether they will stay together, collect a handful of the mixture and squeeze it into a ball with your fist. Open your hand, and if the ingredients are firmly together, proceed with making fritters. Scoop out 4 heaping tablespoons (or approximately 1 fistful) of the mixture and form a patty with your hands. Continue on until all the fritters are made. Set them aside while you finish the rest of the recipe.

3. **Prepare the turmeric yogurt:** In a bowl, combine the yogurt, 2–3 tablespoons water, juice from 1 lemon, turmeric powder, and salt. The yogurt should be a drizzling consistency. If needed, add a splash or two more of water. Whisk until completely combined. Taste and season with salt and pepper.

4. **Prepare the cabbage slaw:** In a bowl, combine the juice from 1 lemon, maple syrup, and remaining water and whisk until smooth. Add the cabbage and red pepper. Thinly slice your remaining shallot into wedges and add that in as well. Season with salt and pepper. Use your hands to combine and massage the dressing into the cabbage. Set aside.

5. **Fry the fritters:** Heat the avocado oil in a wide skillet over medium heat. Add the fritters, in batches, and cook for 4 to 5 minutes per side until golden and crispy. Transfer to a paper towel-lined plate.

6. **To serve:** Spoon the yogurt onto plates and smooth into a circular shape with your spoon. Place a fritter on top and pile the cabbage slaw on top. Garnish with a few additional cilantro leaves and flaky sea salt, if desired. Enjoy!

Black Pepper Tofu in Sesame-Miso Broth

Time to Make: 45 minutes (15 minutes inactive)

Serves: 4

WHY THIS RECIPE WORKS

Tofu is coated with plenty of black pepper and braised to perfection in this creamy sesame-miso broth. Ladled over cooked rice and topped with a crispy peanut garnish, this meal is a perfect blend of peppery richness.

SUBSTITUTIONS

Extra-firm tofu: Seitan, mushrooms, or cubed eggplant
Cassava flour: Arrowroot powder, tapioca flour, or coconut flour
White miso: Red miso
Unsalted peanuts: Almonds, walnuts, cashews, or macadamia nuts

EQUIPMENT & LEFTOVERS

You'll need: Paper towels, heavy object to press the tofu, 2 small pots, and wide pot
Leftovers: Store in an airtight container in the fridge for 3 days

INGREDIENTS

1 pound extra-firm tofu

1 cup uncooked white rice

2 cups water

Salt to taste

2 tablespoons cassava flour plus more as needed

1–2 tablespoons freshly cracked black pepper or more to taste

2 tablespoons + 1 teaspoon avocado oil

1 yellow onion, peeled and thinly sliced into half-moons

6 scallions, minced, divided

2 tablespoons white miso paste

6 cups vegetable stock

2 tablespoons tahini

2 teaspoons sesame oil

2 teaspoons soy sauce

5 ounces baby spinach

1 cup unsalted peanuts

1 tablespoon sesame seeds

(Continued on page 66)

METHOD

1. **Press the tofu:** Wrap the tofu in paper towels and place a heavy object (like a book) on top. Allow the tofu to press for 20 minutes, then cut crosswise into 1-inch slices and cut the block once lengthwise to create equal sized squares.

2. **Cook the rice:** Combine the rice with water and a sprinkle of salt in a small pot. Bring to a boil, then reduce heat and cover for 15 minutes. Turn off the heat and rest for 10 minutes, then remove the lid and fluff the rice with a fork.

3. **Prepare the tofu:** Place the tofu on a plate and dust with cassava flour on each side. Season with salt and black pepper.

4. **Fry the tofu:** Heat 1 tablespoon avocado oil in a wide pot over medium-high heat. Add the tofu in an even layer and cook without moving for 4 to 5 minutes until crisp and browned. Flip and cook for an additional 4 to 5 minutes. Remove the tofu and transfer to a plate. Wipe out the pot.

5. **Cook the aromatics:** Add 1 teaspoon avocado oil to the pot. Add the onion and cook for 5 minutes over medium heat. Add the scallion whites and cook for 4 minutes more. Add the white miso paste, pressing it into the onions, for 1 minute until fragrant.

6. **Season the broth:** Pour in the vegetable stock, stirring to incorporate it into the miso. Once the broth begins to bubble lightly, turn the heat to low and add the tahini, sesame oil, and soy sauce and whisk to incorporate.

7. **Simmer the tofu:** Add the tofu to the broth and cook, uncovered, for 15 minutes.

8. **Finish the broth:** Stir in the spinach and cook for 5 minutes until bright green and wilted. Taste and season to your preferences.

9. **Prepare the peanut garnish:** In a small pot, heat remaining avocado oil over medium heat. Once hot, add the peanuts and cook for 1 to 2 minutes until they begin to turn golden brown. Be careful not to burn them! Turn off the heat and stir in the scallion greens and sesame seeds. Allow to rest for 5 minutes.

10. **To serve:** Divide the cooked rice between bowls and ladle the black pepper tofu and broth on top. Scatter the peanuts across each dish.

Shredded Mushroom Tacos

Time to Make: 40 minutes

Serves: 4

WHY THIS RECIPE WORKS

King oyster (also known as king trumpet) mushrooms are simply amazing shredded and served as tacos. Topped with a spicy Brussels sprouts slaw, these tacos are going to become your new taco night go-to.

SUBSTITUTIONS

King trumpet mushrooms: Any mushroom will work here; simply chop or tear them depending on the variety
Shitake mushrooms: Any mushroom variety, such as cremini, baby bella, oyster, or maitake
Brussels sprouts: Red cabbage or savoy cabbage

EQUIPMENT & LEFTOVERS

You'll need: Baking sheet, small pot, and skillet
Leftovers: Store in an airtight container in the fridge for 3 days

INGREDIENTS

6 king trumpet mushrooms

8 ounces shitake mushrooms, caps thinly sliced

3–4 tablespoons + 1 teaspoon avocado oil, divided

2 teaspoons cumin powder

3 teaspoons chili powder, divided

Salt and pepper to taste

2 tablespoons vegan mayonnaise

2 limes, juiced

1–2 tablespoons maple syrup plus more if desired

Splash of water if needed

10 ounces Brussels sprouts, thinly sliced or shredded

1 red onion, divided

½ cup loosely packed cilantro, finely chopped

1 jalapeño, minced

4 cloves garlic, minced

1 (7-ounce) can hot green chili peppers

1 (15-ounce) can black beans, drained

For Serving

12 small corn tortilla shells

Salt and pepper to taste

(Continued on page 69)

METHOD

1. **Preheat oven to 400°F.**

2. **Shred the king trumpet mushrooms:** Cut any woody ends off the bottoms of the mushrooms. Use a fork to shred down the entire length of the mushroom. Make several long shreds down the mushroom until you're able to pull it apart. Pull the mushrooms apart with your fingers. Break the caps into small pieces.

3. **Roast the mushrooms:** Arrange the shredded trumpet and sliced shitake mushroom caps on a baking sheet. Toss with the 2 tablespoons avocado oil, cumin powder, 2 teaspoons chili powder, salt, and pepper. Transfer to the oven and roast for 20 to 25 minutes. Turn off the heat and leave the mushrooms in the warm oven.

4. **Make the Brussels sprouts slaw:** In a small bowl mix together the vegan mayonnaise, lime juice, maple syrup, remaining chili powder, and 1–2 tablespoons avocado oil until smooth. Add a splash or two of water to thin it out. The dressing should be smooth but not too thin. Mince ½ red onion and combine it in a separate bowl with the Brussels sprouts, cilantro, and jalapeño. Season with salt and pepper. Pour the dressing over the Brussels sprouts and toss to coat. Set aside.

5. **Prepare the black beans:** In a small pot, heat remaining avocado oil over medium heat. Slice the remaining red onion into wedges and add to the pot. Cook for 5 minutes. Add the garlic and cook for 1 minute. Add the green chili peppers and the black beans. Season with salt and pepper. Reduce heat and simmer for 15 minutes. Taste and season again before serving.

6. **To serve:** Warm the tortillas in a dry skillet or over an open flame for 30 to 45 seconds per side. Arrange the tortillas on plates and add a spoonful of beans to each tortilla. Pile the mushrooms on top and garnish with the slaw. Serve with more limes and a few cilantro leaves, if desired. Enjoy!

PLAN 2: WEEK 1

This recipe plan includes dinner recipes for five days, all of which serve four. To conquer the grocery store in one shopping trip, the next page outlines a detailed grocery list, with items separated by store department. You will also find storage, freezing, and thawing tips to help you plan your week. This plan is all about the crunchy garnishes! Pay special attention to the key players throughout the week (unsalted almonds, fresh parsley, and escarole) and be sure to buy the freshest and healthiest of those ingredients that you can find because you will use them for multiple recipes.

THE MENU

MONDAY
Lentils in Caramelized Shallot Broth
with Smoky Almonds

TUESDAY
Harissa Roasted Vegetables with Za'atar
Whipped Cauliflower

WEDNESDAY
Wild Mushroom Pasta with Almonds
and Capers

THURSDAY
Greens and Beans with Olives

FRIDAY
Jammy Tomato Udon

PLAN 2: WEEK 1
CONQUERING THE GROCERY STORE

FOOD SAFETY GUIDELINES

Buying groceries for the entire week can require some forethought, so be sure to refer to the FDA's storage and freezing guidelines for your ingredients. To keep herbs and leafy greens fresh through the week, wrap them in a damp paper towel and store in a bag in your crisper. Refresh the paper towel periodically through the week to keep them extra fresh.

OIL
- ☐ Avocado oil
- ☐ Extra-virgin olive oil

PLANT-BASED DAIRY
- ☐ ½ cup (4 ounces) plain cashew milk or plain almond milk Greek yogurt
- ☐ 6 tablespoons plant-based butter

STOCK
- ☐ 15 cups vegetable stock
- ☐ ½ cup white wine (or vegetable stock)

FRUITS & VEGETABLES
- ☐ 3 yellow onions
- ☐ 7 shallots
- ☐ 1½ pounds mixed mushrooms
- ☐ 1½ pounds cauliflower florets
- ☐ 1 head + 6 cloves garlic
- ☐ 1 red Fresno chili pepper
- ☐ 2 Thai chili peppers, optional
- ☐ 4 small zucchini
- ☐ 1 pound broccolini
- ☐ 4 small carrots
- ☐ 2 heads escarole
- ☐ 5 ounces baby spinach
- ☐ 4 Roma tomatoes
- ☐ 1 pint cherry tomatoes
- ☐ 1 lemon

- ☐ 10 scallions
- ☐ 2 cups parsley
- ☐ ¼ cup fresh dill

PANTRY & SPICES
- ☐ 1 (15-ounce) can chickpeas
- ☐ 2 (15-ounce) cans cannellini beans
- ☐ 16 ounces French green lentils
- ☐ 16 ounces linguine
- ☐ 16 ounces fresh or frozen udon noodles
- ☐ 1½ cups thinly sliced unsalted almonds
- ☐ 1 cup raw pumpkin seeds
- ☐ 3 tablespoons (½ ounce) capers
- ☐ 1 cup Castelvetrano pitted olives
- ☐ Soy sauce
- ☐ Chili oil
- ☐ Sesame oil
- ☐ Sesame seeds
- ☐ Sugar, optional
- ☐ Smoked paprika
- ☐ Harissa powder
- ☐ Za'atar seasoning
- ☐ Garlic powder
- ☐ Dry thyme
- ☐ Salt
- ☐ Pepper
- ☐ White pepper
- ☐ Crushed red pepper

Lentils in Caramelized Shallot Broth with Smoky Almonds

Time to Make: 60 minutes (20 minutes inactive)

Serves: 4

WHY THIS RECIPE WORKS

This recipe is smoky, sweet, and filling. Topped with a crispy almond and caramelized shallot garnish, these lentils are big on flavor. You will have leftover almond oil which can be used as a finishing oil in tomorrow's recipe.

SUBSTITUTIONS

French green lentils: Black lentils or brown lentils
Unsalted almonds: Unsalted peanuts or unsalted cashews

EQUIPMENT & LEFTOVERS

You'll need: Large pot, colander, small pot, and wide pot
Leftovers: Store Lentils in Caramelized Shallot Broth with Smoky Almonds in an airtight container in the fridge for 3 days and store leftover almond oil in an airtight jar in the fridge for 7 days

INGREDIENTS

16 ounces French green lentils

Salt and pepper to taste

½ cup + 1 tablespoon avocado oil, divided

1 cup thinly sliced unsalted almonds

6 large shallots, peeled and thinly sliced

1 teaspoon sugar, optional

6 cups vegetable stock

1 cup fresh parsley, minced

6 scallions, minced

2 teaspoons smoked paprika

METHOD

1. **Cook the lentils:** Combine 6 cups water with the green lentils in a large pot. Bring to a boil, then reduce heat to low. Simmer, partially covered, for 20 to 25 minutes until tender. Drain, rinse, and season with salt.

2. **Prepare the almond oil:** Combine ½ cup avocado oil and the almonds in a small pot. Turn the heat to medium, then reduce heat to low. Simmer for 15 minutes until the almonds are golden brown. Strain the oil into a heat-proof container. Transfer the cooked almonds to a bowl and sprinkle with salt.

3. **Caramelize the shallots:** Heat remaining avocado oil in a wide pot over medium heat. Add the shallots. Season with salt, pepper, and the sugar (if using). Cook, stirring often, for 20 to 30 minutes until completely caramelized. Be careful not to burn the shallots, and adjust the heat as necessary. Turn off the heat, scoop out half the caramelized shallots, and transfer to the bowl with the almonds. Leave the remaining shallots in the pan.

4. **Cook the broth:** Return the pan with the shallots to medium heat. Pour in the stock and bring to a boil. Reduce heat and simmer for 5 to 10 minutes. Taste and season with salt and pepper.

5. **Finish the broth:** Stir in the parsley and scallions and cook for 5 minutes more. Turn off the heat.

6. **Finish the almond garnish:** To the bowl of almonds and caramelized shallots, add the smoked paprika, and toss to combine. Set aside.

7. **To serve:** Divide the cooked lentils between bowls. Ladle the hot broth on top and garnish with the crispy almond garnish. Drizzle with a teaspoon or two of the reserved almond oil. Enjoy!

Harissa Roasted Vegetables with Za'atar Whipped Cauliflower

Time to Make: 45 minutes (15 minutes inactive)

Serves: 4

WHY THIS RECIPE WORKS

Roasting zucchini without salt allows it to crisp up and char rather than wilt. Served over a flavorful za'atar mashed cauliflower, this dinner is easy, fast, and flavorful. If your zucchini is quite large, use two baking sheets—one for the zucchini and one for the broccolini and chickpeas—and be sure to double the harissa powder and oil.

SUBSTITUTIONS

Zucchini: Eggplant or yellow squash
Broccolini: Broccoli florets or broccoli rabe

EQUIPMENT & LEFTOVERS

You'll need: Large pot, baking sheet, colander, and immersion blender or hand mixer
Leftovers: Store in an airtight container in the fridge for 3 days

INGREDIENTS

1½ pounds cauliflower florets

1 teaspoon salt plus more to taste

4 small zucchini, cut into angled wedges

1 pound broccolini

1 (15-ounce) can chickpeas, drained

1 tablespoon avocado oil

1 tablespoon harissa powder plus more for serving

Pepper to taste

1 tablespoon za'atar seasoning

1 teaspoon garlic powder

½ cup plain cashew milk yogurt or plain almond milk Greek yogurt plus more as needed

Homemade almond oil, for garnish, optional

Crushed red pepper, for garnish, optional

METHOD

1. **Preheat oven to 425°F.**

2. **Start the whipped cauliflower:** Place the cauliflower in a large pot and cover with water. Add the salt. Bring to a boil and cook for 20 minutes until completely tender. Drain and return to the pot. Set aside until needed.

3. **Roast the vegetables:** Arrange the zucchini on half the baking sheet. Arrange the broccolini on the other half. Pour the chickpeas over the entire baking sheet. Drizzle the oil over the vegetables and use your hands to coat the vegetables. Sprinkle the harissa powder over all of the ingredients on the baking sheet and transfer to the oven for 15 minutes. If desired, broil for 3 to 4 minutes to char the tops of the zucchini. Turn off the heat and sprinkle salt and pepper over everything on the baking sheet.

4. **Prepare the whipped cauliflower:** Return the pot of cooked cauliflower to the stove over low heat. Sprinkle the cauliflower with za'atar, garlic powder, salt, and pepper to taste. Add the yogurt to the pot and toss to combine. Use an immersion blender or hand mixer to blend until smooth and creamy, adding more yogurt as necessary until your desired consistency is met. Taste and season with salt and pepper. Keep warm.

5. **To serve:** Divide the whipped cauliflower between plates and pile the roasted vegetables and chickpeas on top. Drizzle with the homemade almond oil from yesterday and a sprinkle of crushed red pepper or more harissa powder. Enjoy!

Wild Mushroom Pasta with Almonds and Capers

Time to Make: 40 minutes

Serves: 4

WHY THIS RECIPE WORKS

Use the rest of your almonds in this briny, crunchy topping. It pairs beautifully with the wild mushrooms and the bitter escarole. If you cannot find foraged mushrooms, like maitake or chanterelles, use any mushroom variety you like. Cremini or shitake will also work wonderfully in this recipe.

SUBSTITUTIONS

Almonds: Crushed cashews or walnuts
Linguine: Your favorite pasta
Escarole: Radicchio or baby spinach

EQUIPMENT & LEFTOVERS

You'll need: Wide pot, large pot, and colander
Leftovers: Store in an airtight container in the fridge for 3 days

INGREDIENTS

2 teaspoons avocado oil

1 shallot, peeled and thinly sliced into rounds

½ cup sliced almonds

3 tablespoons capers, drained

½ cup fresh parsley leaves, minced

Salt and pepper to taste

16 ounces linguine

2 tablespoons extra-virgin olive oil

1 yellow onion, peeled and thinly sliced into half-moons

3 tablespoons plant-based butter

1½ pounds mixed mushrooms, sliced, diced, or torn depending on variety

½ cup white wine or vegetable stock

1 head escarole, roughly chopped

METHOD

1. **Prepare the almond and caper garnish:** In a wide pot, heat the avocado oil over medium heat. Add the shallot and cook for 2 to 3 minutes until it just begins to soften. Continue cooking until the edges turn golden brown. Be careful not to burn the shallot. Add the almonds and cook for 1 to 2 minutes until just beginning to toast. Turn the heat to medium high and add the capers. Cook, tossing regularly, for 2 to 3 minutes more until the almonds are golden brown. Turn off the heat and immediately transfer to a bowl. Wipe out the pot and reserve for the wild mushroom sauce. Add the minced parsley to the bowl of almonds and toss to combine. Season with salt and set aside.

2. **Cook the pasta:** Bring a large pot of salted water to a boil. Once boiling, add the pasta and cook until al dente. Reserve ¾ cup of the pasta cooking water and drain the pasta. Set aside.

3. **While you wait for the pasta water to boil, prepare the mushroom sauce in the same pot you used to make the almond garnish:** Heat the extra-virgin olive oil in the pot over medium heat. Add the onion and cook for 4 to 5 minutes. Melt the plant-based butter into the pot and add the mushrooms. Cook for 12 to 15 minutes until the mushrooms crisp up and turn a deep golden brown. Season with salt and pepper.

(Continued on next page)

4. **Finish the wild mushroom sauce:** Add the white wine or vegetable stock to the pot and bring to a boil. Cook for 5 minutes. Stir in ½ cup of the pasta cooking water and bring to a boil for 5 to 6 minutes until reduced slightly. Turn the heat to low and add the escarole. Cook until just wilted, about 4 minutes. Season again with salt and pepper. If the sauce reduces too much, add the remaining ¼ cup pasta cooking water.

5. **Finish the pasta:** Add the cooked pasta to the pot of mushroom sauce and toss to coat. Cook for 1 to 2 minutes until glossy. Turn off the heat.

6. **To serve:** Divide the pasta between plates and scatter the almond caper garnish on top of each plate. Enjoy!

Greens and Beans with Olives

Time to Make: 55 minutes

Serves: 4

WHY THIS RECIPE WORKS

Greens, beans, and olives make for a dream team in this easy-to-prepare soup. A bitter green like escarole stands up well to the salty, briny flavor from the olives.

SUBSTITUTIONS

Red Fresno chili pepper: Your favorite hot pepper, such as habanero, jalapeño, or serrano, or crushed red pepper to taste
Castelvetrano olives: Your favorite green or black olive variety
Escarole: Baby spinach, arugula, or baby kale

EQUIPMENT & LEFTOVERS

You'll need: Large pot and food processor
Leftovers: Store in an airtight container in the fridge for 3 days

INGREDIENTS

2 teaspoons avocado oil

1 yellow onion, peeled and diced

4 small carrots, peeled and small-diced

Salt and pepper to taste

1 head garlic, peeled

3 tablespoons plant-based butter

1 red Fresno chili pepper

2 teaspoons dry thyme

¼ teaspoon crushed red pepper

¼ teaspoon white pepper

8 cups vegetable stock

2 (15-ounce) cans cannellini beans

½ cup fresh parsley, loosely packed

¼ cup fresh dill

2 tablespoons Castelvetrano olive brine + 1 cup pitted olives, divided

1 lemon, juiced

¼ cup extra-virgin olive oil

1 head escarole

(Continued on page 81)

METHOD

1. **Cook the onion and carrots:** Heat the avocado oil in a large pot over medium-high heat. Add the diced onion and cook for 6 to 8 minutes until it begins to soften and turn golden brown. Add the carrots and cook for an additional 7 to 8 minutes until they begin to soften. Season lightly with salt and pepper.

2. **Prepare the garlic:** Transfer the garlic to a food processor and pulse until completely minced. Remove all but 1 teaspoon from the food processor (leave the remaining teaspoon in the processor).

3. **Cook the aromatics:** Melt the plant-based butter into the pot of onions and carrots, then add the garlic and the red Fresno chili pepper. Cook for 45 seconds. Add the dry thyme, crushed red pepper, and white pepper and cook for 1 minute until fragrant.

4. **Simmer the soup:** Pour in the vegetable stock and bring to a boil. Stir in the drained beans and season with salt and pepper. Simmer for 30 minutes. Taste and season again to your preferences.

5. **Prepare the garnish:** To the food processor with the remaining garlic, add the parsley, dill, olive brine, lemon juice and extra-virgin olive oil. Pulse until combined. If it's too thick, add a touch more oil or a splash of water. Taste and season with salt. Set aside.

6. **Finish the greens and beans:** Add the olives to the broth. Leave some whole and pinch some between your fingers as you add them to broth to break them in half or into pieces. Stir in the escarole and cook until bright green and just wilted. Taste and season once more. Turn off the heat.

7. **To serve:** Ladle the greens and beans into bowls and spoon the herb garnish on top. Enjoy!

Jammy Tomato Udon

Time to Make: 60 minutes (20 minutes inactive)

Serves: 4

WHY THIS RECIPE WORKS

Big noodles deserve big flavor. And this Jammy Tomato Udon delivers on all fronts. The jammy tomatoes stick well to the udon to give you that spicy sweetness with every slurp. Topped with chili oil-soaked pumpkin seeds, this bowl of udon is an explosion of flavor.

SUBSTITUTIONS

Udon noodles: Soba or ramen (cook time may very)
Baby spinach: Baby kale or chopped dandelion greens
Chili oil: Avocado oil

EQUIPMENT & LEFTOVERS

You'll need: Wide pot, small pot, large pot, and colander
Leftovers: Store in an airtight container in the fridge for 3 days

INGREDIENTS

1 tablespoon avocado oil

1 yellow onion, peeled and thinly sliced into half-moons

4 Roma tomatoes

1 pint cherry tomatoes

Salt and pepper to taste

6 cloves garlic, peeled and minced

2 Thai chili peppers, minced, optional

4 scallions, minced, divided

1 tablespoon soy sauce

1 tablespoon sesame oil

2 teaspoons sugar

1 cup vegetable stock

½ cup chili oil

1 cup raw pumpkin seeds

1 teaspoon sesame seeds

16 ounces fresh or frozen udon noodles

5 ounces baby spinach

(Continued on next page)

METHOD

1. **Start the tomato sauce:** Heat the avocado oil in a wide pot over medium-high heat. Add the onion and the Roma and cherry tomatoes and cook for 7 to 10 minutes until softened and beginning to char. Season with salt. Add the minced garlic, Thai chili peppers (if using), and white parts of the scallions and cook for 1 minute until fragrant.

2. **Simmer the sauce:** Add the soy sauce, sesame oil, and sugar. Pour in the vegetable stock and bring to a boil. Taste and season to your preferences. Reduce heat to medium low and simmer, uncovered, for 20 to 30 minutes. If the sauce reduces too quickly, turn the heat to very low and add a splash of water.

3. **Prepare the chili oil-soaked pumpkin seeds:** Combine the chili oil and pumpkin seeds in a small pot and turn the heat to low. Cook the pumpkin seeds in the oil for 20 minutes, stirring occasionally. Turn off the heat and stir in the green parts of the scallions. Add 1 teaspoon sesame seeds.

4. **Cook the noodles:** Cook the udon noodles in a large pot according to package instructions. Drain, rinse, and set aside.

5. **Cook the spinach:** Add the spinach to the tomato sauce and cook for 3 to 4 minutes until wilted.

6. **Finish the udon:** Add the udon to the sauce and toss to coat until the udon is warmed through. Add 2 tablespoons of the chili oil-soaked pumpkin seeds to the udon and toss to coat. Turn off the heat.

7. **To serve:** Divide the udon between bowls. Spoon a teaspoon or two of the pumpkin seeds on top of each dish.

PLAN 2: WEEK 2

This recipe plan includes dinner recipes for five days, all of which serve four. To conquer the grocery store in one shopping trip, the next page outlines a detailed grocery list, with items separated by store department. You will also find storage, freezing, and thawing tips to help you plan your week. This plan is all about sweet and heat! Pay special attention to the key players throughout the week (sweet potatoes and green beans) and be sure to buy the freshest and healthiest of those ingredients that you can find, because you will use them for multiple recipes.

THE MENU

MONDAY
Kimchi Tteokguk with Pickled
Vegetables

TUESDAY
Harissa Chickpea Soup with Coconut

WEDNESDAY
Sweet Potato Confit with Lentils

THURSDAY
Moroccan-Spiced Rice and
Chickpeas

FRIDAY
Roasted Carrots with Carrot Top
Chimichurri

PLAN 2: WEEK 2

CONQUERING THE GROCERY STORE

FOOD SAFETY GUIDELINES

Buying groceries for the entire week can require some forethought, so be sure to refer to the FDA's storage and freezing guidelines for your ingredients. To keep herbs and leafy greens fresh through the week, wrap them in a damp paper towel and store in a bag in your crisper. Refresh the paper towel periodically through the week to keep them extra fresh.

PLANT-BASED PROTEIN
- ☐ 1 pound extra-firm tofu

GRAINS
- ☐ 1 cup uncooked white rice

OIL
- ☐ Avocado oil
- ☐ Extra-virgin olive oil

PLANT-BASED DAIRY
- ☐ ½ cup plant-based Greek yogurt

STOCK
- ☐ 10 cups vegetable stock

FRUITS & VEGETABLES
- ☐ 3 yellow onions
- ☐ 1 shallot
- ☐ 14 cloves garlic
- ☐ 2 pounds sweet potatoes
- ☐ 3 small scarlet turnips
- ☐ 4 golden beets
- ☐ 1 jalapeño pepper
- ☐ 1 red Fresno chili pepper
- ☐ 1 daikon radish
- ☐ 1 bunch carrots with leafy green tops
- ☐ 3 ounces baby spinach
- ☐ 4 ounces watercress
- ☐ 1 head little gem lettuce
- ☐ 1 zucchini
- ☐ 20 ounces green beans
- ☐ 1 pound asparagus
- ☐ 2 pints cherry tomatoes
- ☐ ½ cup dried apricots
- ☐ 8 ounces pomegranate seeds
- ☐ 1 lime
- ☐ 1 orange
- ☐ 6 scallions
- ☐ 1 cup parsley

PANTRY & SPICES

- ☐ 3 (15-ounce) cans chickpeas
- ☐ 1 (14-ounce) jar store-bought kimchi
- ☐ 1 (15-ounce) can light coconut milk
- ☐ 1 cup black lentils
- ☐ 1 pound store-bought rice cakes (tteok)
- ☐ Distilled white vinegar
- ☐ Red wine vinegar
- ☐ White sugar
- ☐ Soy sauce

- ☐ Sesame oil
- ☐ Gochugaru
- ☐ Ras el hanout
- ☐ Harissa powder
- ☐ Harissa paste
- ☐ Chili powder
- ☐ Paprika
- ☐ Cayenne powder, optional
- ☐ Flaky sea salt
- ☐ Salt
- ☐ Pepper

Kimchi Tteokguk with Pickled Vegetables

Time to Make: 45 minutes (20 minutes inactive)

Serves: 4

WHY THIS RECIPE WORKS

Tteokguk is a Korean rice cake soup traditionally eaten during the celebration of the Korean New Year to bring good luck. Kimchi tteokguk is a rice cake soup prepared with kimchi as its base ingredient. This recipe is an homage to the original. Pickled vegetables add a sweet, tangy flavor to cut through the heat of the kimchi.

SUBSTITUTIONS

Rice cakes (tteok): If you cannot find rice cakes, simply omit and serve the soup with cooked white rice on the side
Daikon radish: Red radishes

EQUIPMENT & LEFTOVERS

You'll need: Large pot, small pot, paper towels, and heavy object to press the tofu
Leftovers: Store the broth in an airtight container in the fridge for 3–4 days and reheat leftovers on the stove, adding more rice cakes as you intend to eat them, and store the pickled vegetables in an airtight container in the fridge for 2 days

INGREDIENTS

1 pound extra-firm tofu

1 tablespoon avocado oil

1 yellow onion, peeled and thinly sliced into half-moons

4 cloves garlic, peeled and minced

6 scallions, minced, divided

1 tablespoon gochugaru or crushed red pepper to taste

1 (14-ounce) jar store-bought kimchi

6 cups vegetable stock

2 tablespoons soy sauce

1 tablespoon sesame oil

Salt and pepper to taste

1 cup water

½ cup distilled white vinegar

¼ cup white sugar

3 ounces baby spinach

1 daikon radish, peeled and thinly sliced

1 pound store-bought rice cakes (tteok)

(Continued on next page)

METHOD

1. **Press the tofu:** Wrap the tofu in paper towels and place a heavy object (like a book) on top. Allow the tofu to press for 10 to 15 minutes before slicing into 2-inch cubes.

2. **Start the soup:** Heat the avocado oil in a large pot over medium-high heat. Add the onion and cook for 5 minutes until it begins to soften. Add the minced garlic and white parts of the scallions and cook for 1 minute until fragrant. Sprinkle the gochugaru or crushed red pepper over the aromatics and cook for 1 minute. Add kimchi and toss to combine. Cook for 2 minutes.

3. **Simmer the soup:** Pour in the vegetable stock, soy sauce, and sesame oil. Bring to a boil. Reduce heat and simmer, uncovered, for 25 minutes. Taste and season to your preferences.

4. **Prepare the pickled vegetables:** Combine the water, vinegar, and sugar in a small pot. Bring to a boil. As soon as the sugar has dissolved, turn off the heat. In a large heat-proof bowl or large mason jar, toss the spinach, daikon radish, and green parts of the scallion. Pour the vinegar mixture over the vegetables. Season with salt to taste. Set aside.

5. **Finish the soup:** Bring the soup back to a low boil. Add the tteok and cook for 3 minutes until they are almost tender. Add the tofu and cook for 5 minutes until the tofu is warmed through and the tteok have floated to the top and are softened (but not soggy!). Taste and adjust to your preferences.

6. **To serve:** Ladle the kimchi tteokguk into bowls. Spoon the pickled vegetables on top. Enjoy!

Harissa Chickpea Soup with Coconut

Time to Make: 50 minutes (30 minutes inactive)

Serves: 4

WHY THIS RECIPE WORKS

This harissa chickpea soup with coconut is smoky, sweet, and so easy to make. Topped with a charred vegetable salad, it's an amazing combination of flavors. The charred vegetables are served warm on top of the soup and give it a perfect tender-crisp bite.

SUBSTITUTIONS

Sweet potato: Butternut or acorn squash
Green beans: Broccoli florets or sugar snap peas
Zucchini: Yellow squash or eggplant

EQUIPMENT & LEFTOVERS

You'll need: Large pot and baking sheet
Leftovers: Store in an airtight container in the fridge for 3 days

INGREDIENTS

2 teaspoons avocado oil

1 yellow onion, peeled and diced

1 pound sweet potatoes, peeled and small-diced

2 (15-ounce) cans chickpeas, drained

Salt and pepper to taste

1 tablespoon harissa powder

2 teaspoons chili powder

2 teaspoons paprika

½ teaspoon cayenne powder, more or less to taste, optional

4 cups vegetable stock

½ cup fresh parsley leaves, minced

1 jalapeño, minced

1 lime, juiced

12 ounces green beans, broken in half

1 zucchini, diced

1 tablespoon extra-virgin olive oil

1 (15-ounce) can light coconut milk

(Continued on page 93)

METHOD

1. **Start the soup:** Heat the avocado oil in a large pot over medium heat. Add the onion and cook, stirring regularly, for 7 to 8 minutes until it softens. Add the sweet potatoes and cook, stirring regularly, for 7 minutes until it begins to brown around the edges. Add the chickpeas and toss briefly until just warmed. Season everything in the pot with salt and pepper. Add the harissa powder, chili powder, paprika, and cayenne (if using) and cook for 45 seconds until fragrant.

2. **Simmer the soup:** Pour in the vegetable stock and bring to a boil. Reduce heat and simmer for 30 minutes until reduced and thickened. Taste and season to your preferences.

3. **As the soup simmers, prepare the charred vegetables:** In a bowl, combine the parsley, jalapeño, and lime juice and season with salt. Set aside and turn the broiler on. Arrange the green beans and zucchini on a baking sheet and drizzle with olive oil. Season with salt and pepper. Transfer to the broiler and cook for 3 to 5 minutes. It may take longer depending on your broiler. Keep an eye on the vegetables. Once the green beans and zucchini char around the edges, remove them from the broiler. They should still be bright green. Add the charred vegetables to the bowl of lime juice and parsley and toss to coat. Taste and season to your preferences.

4. **Finish the soup:** Add the coconut milk to the soup and cook for an additional 10 minutes.

5. **To serve:** Ladle the soup into bowls and pile the charred vegetables on top. Enjoy!

Sweet Potato Confit with Lentils

Time to Make: 60 minutes (30 minutes inactive)

Serves: 4

WHY THIS RECIPE WORKS

Sweet potatoes take on a luxurious texture when they are cooked slowly in oil. Paired with blanched asparagus and a very simple citrus salt, this meal will transform your Wednesday dinner into an extraordinary dining experience. The reserved confit oil can be used as a finishing oil in other recipes.

SUBSTITUTIONS

Sweet potato: Butternut or acorn squash
Cherry tomatoes: Quartered Roma tomatoes or other vegetable like baby carrots or parsnips
Orange: Lemon
Black lentils: French green lentils

EQUIPMENT & LEFTOVERS

You'll need: Large shallow baking dish, large pot, tongs, and colander
Leftovers: Store the Sweet Potato Confit with Lentils in an airtight container in the fridge for 3 days and store any extra citrus salt in a separate container (allow citrus salt to dry in the open air before storing) for 3 months

INGREDIENTS

1 pound (2 whole) sweet potatoes, cut into ¾-inch rounds

1 shallot, peeled and sliced into wedges

1 pint cherry tomatoes

½ cup extra-virgin olive oil, plus more as needed

Salt and pepper to taste

1 orange, juiced and zested, divided

2 tablespoons flaky sea salt

1 pound asparagus, woody ends trimmed

1 cup black lentils

METHOD

1. **Preheat oven to 350°.**

2. **Prepare the sweet potato confit:** Arrange the sweet potatoes in a large shallow baking dish. Place the shallots and tomatoes on top and season liberally with salt and pepper. Pour ½ cup extra-virgin olive oil to start. Continue adding oil until the vegetables are nearly covered. It's okay if the tops are a little exposed, but the potatoes and tomatoes should be nearly submerged. Transfer to the oven and bake for 50 to 60 minutes until the tops of the sweet potatoes are golden. Turn off the heat.

3. **Prepare the citrus salt:** In a bowl, combine the orange zest and flaky sea salt and mix until completely combined. Set out at room temperature as you finish the recipe.

4. **About 20 minutes before the sweet potatoes finish baking, cook the asparagus and lentils:** Bring a large pot of water to a boil. Add the asparagus and cook for 1 to 3 minutes until bright green. Using tongs, transfer the asparagus to a bowl of ice water. Leave the water boiling on the stove. To the boiling water, add the black lentils and cook for 15 to 20 minutes until tender. Drain and rinse the lentils and transfer to a bowl. Drizzle with extra-virgin olive oil, a sprinkle of salt, and orange juice and toss to coat.

5. **To serve:** Divide cooked lentils between shallow bowls and arrange the confit vegetables on top. Place the blanched asparagus on top of each dish and sprinkle it with citrus salt. Enjoy!

Moroccan-Spiced Rice and Chickpeas

Time to Make: 35 minutes

Serves: 4

WHY THIS RECIPE WORKS

Ras el hanout is the dominant flavor in this easy, dreamy weeknight dinner. Paired with bright pomegranate seeds and a crisp lettuce garnish, this meal is equal parts warming and bright.

SUBSTITUTIONS

Ras el hanout: If you cannot find ras el hanout, prepare a similar spice mix using this recipe: 1 teaspoon cumin powder, 1 teaspoon ground cardamom, 1 teaspoon ground ginger, ½ teaspoon ground cinnamon, ½ teaspoon ground coriander, ½ teaspoon ground allspice, ½ teaspoon ground cloves, and a dash cayenne pepper, optional

Little gem lettuce: Romaine lettuce

Pomegranate seeds: Halved grapes

EQUIPMENT & LEFTOVERS

You'll need: Small pot and skillet

Leftovers: Store rice and chickpeas together in an airtight container in the fridge for 3 days and store lettuce garnish in a separate container in the fridge for up to 2 days

INGREDIENTS

3 cups water, divided

Salt and pepper to taste

1 cup uncooked white rice

1 tablespoon avocado oil

1 yellow onion, peeled and finely diced

6 cloves garlic, peeled and minced

1 tablespoon ras el hanout spice mix

1 tablespoon harissa paste

1 (15-ounce) can chickpeas, drained

½ cup dried apricots, diced

1 pint cherry tomatoes, halved

Cayenne powder, optional, to taste

8 ounces fresh green beans, chopped roughly

1 head little gem lettuce, thinly sliced

1 tablespoon extra-virgin olive oil

8 ounces pomegranate seeds

(Continued on page 98)

METHOD

1. **Cook the rice:** Add 2 cups water to a small pot and bring to a boil. Add salt and the white rice. Stir once and reduce heat. Cover and cook for 15 minutes. Turn off the heat and allow the rice to rest for 10 minutes, then remove the lid and fluff with a fork.

2. **Prepare the Moroccan-spiced chickpeas:** Heat the avocado oil in a skillet over medium heat. Add onion and cook for 5 to 6 minutes until it just begins to soften. Add the garlic and cook for 1 minute until fragrant. Add ras el hanout and cook for 30 seconds until fragrant. Add the harissa paste and cook for an additional 30 seconds until fragrant. Add chickpeas and toss to coat. Pour in 1 cup water and bring to a boil. Simmer for 5 minutes. Stir in the apricots and cherry tomatoes. Reduce heat and simmer for 15 minutes. Season with salt, pepper, and a little cayenne, if desired. Add a splash of water if the broth reduces too quickly. Taste and season to your preferences. Stir in the green beans and cook for 5 minutes until tender-crisp. Turn off the heat.

3. **Prepare the salad garnish:** Combine lettuce and extra-virgin olive oil. Stir in pomegranate seeds and season with salt and pepper. Set aside.

4. **To serve:** Divide cooked rice between bowls and pile the chickpeas on top. Divide the salad garnish between each bowl. Enjoy!

Roasted Carrots with Carrot Top Chimichurri

Time to Make: 60 minutes (20 minutes inactive)

Serves: 4

WHY THIS RECIPE WORKS

I use the whole carrot in this recipe! Best of all, this carrot top chimichurri is the perfect vehicle for any leftover herbs lurking in your crisper.

SUBSTITUTIONS

Scarlet turnips: 1 white turnip
Red Fresno chili pepper: Jalapeño or habanero pepper
Red wine vinegar: Lemon juice or white wine vinegar
Watercress: Your favorite microgreen or baby spinach, arugula, or baby kale

EQUIPMENT & LEFTOVERS

You'll need: Two baking sheets, medium pot, food processor, and immersion blender or potato masher
Leftovers: Store in an airtight container in the fridge for 3 days

INGREDIENTS

1 bunch carrots, halved, tops reserved for the chimichurri and for garnish

4 tablespoons avocado oil, divided

Salt and pepper to taste

3 small scarlet turnips, very thinly sliced

4 golden beets, peeled and cubed

½ cup plant-based Greek yogurt

½ cup loosely packed parsley leaves

2 tablespoons red wine vinegar

4 cloves garlic, peeled

1 red Fresno chili pepper or crushed red pepper to taste

½ cup extra-virgin olive oil, plus more for garnish

4 ounces watercress

(Continued on page 101)

METHOD

1. **Preheat oven to 425°F.**

2. **Roast the carrots and turnips:** Arrange the halved carrots on one baking sheet. Drizzle and toss with 2 tablespoons avocado oil. Season with salt. On a second baking sheet, arrange the thinly sliced turnips and drizzle with the remaining avocado oil. Season with salt and pepper. Transfer both baking sheets to the oven and roast for 25 minutes, flipping both the carrots and the turnips once halfway through. Remove from the oven and set aside.

3. **Prepare the beet puree:** In a medium pot, cover the beets with water and season liberally with salt. Bring to a boil over high heat. Once boiling, reduce the heat to medium and cook for 20 minutes or until the beets are fork tender. Drain and return to the pot. Use an immersion blender or potato masher to mash the beets. Add the Greek yogurt and continue blending or mashing until smooth. Taste and season with salt and pepper. Keep warm.

4. **Prepare the chimichurri:** Thoroughly rinse the reserved carrot tops and transfer to a food processor with the parsley, red wine vinegar, garlic cloves, and red Fresno chili pepper. Pulse until finely chopped. Slowly pour in the extra-virgin olive oil and continue pulsing for 10 more seconds. Pour the chimichurri into a bowl and season with salt and pepper. Set aside.

5. **To serve:** Divide the warm beet puree between plates. Arrange watercress on top of each plate. Place the turnip chips and roasted carrots on top and spoon the chimichurri across the top. Garnish with a few reserved carrot greens if you have any extra. Drizzle with a touch of extra-virgin olive oil. Enjoy!

PLAN 2: WEEK 3

This recipe plan includes dinner recipes for five days, all of which serve four. To conquer the grocery store in one shopping trip, the next page outlines a detailed grocery list, with items separated by store department. You will also find storage, freezing, and thawing tips to help you plan your week. This plan is all about one of our very favorite aromatic vegetables: celery! This wonderfully versatile vegetable deserves its time to shine. Pay special attention to the key players throughout the week (celery, pears, and asparagus) and be sure to buy the freshest and healthiest of those ingredients that you can find because you will use them for multiple recipes.

THE MENU

MONDAY
Butternut Squash Steak with Fennel-Potato Puree

TUESDAY
Farro and Burst Tomatoes in Celery Broth

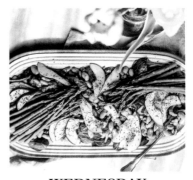

WEDNESDAY
Pear Salad with White Beans and Vegetables

THURSDAY
Fennel Barley Stew with Celery

FRIDAY
Charred Pears with Harissa Chickpeas

PLAN 2: WEEK 3
CONQUERING THE GROCERY STORE

FOOD SAFETY GUIDELINES
Buying groceries for the entire week can require some forethought, so be sure to refer to the FDA's storage and freezing guidelines for your ingredients. To keep herbs and leafy greens fresh through the week, wrap them in a damp paper towel and store in a bag in your crisper. Refresh the paper towel periodically through the week to keep them extra fresh.

GRAINS
- ☐ 1 cup farro
- ☐ 1 cup pearl barley

OIL
- ☐ Avocado oil
- ☐ Extra-virgin olive oil

PLANT-BASED DAIRY
- ☐ ¾ cup plant-based Greek yogurt
- ☐ 4 tablespoons plant-based butter

STOCK
- ☐ 14 cups vegetable stock

FRUITS & VEGETABLES
- ☐ 3 yellow onions
- ☐ 1 head garlic
- ☐ 3 fennel bulbs
- ☐ 10 ribs celery with leaves
- ☐ 4 carrots
- ☐ 1½ pounds Yukon Gold potatoes
- ☐ 1 whole butternut squash
- ☐ 6 ounces baby spinach
- ☐ 2 pounds asparagus
- ☐ 2 pints cherry tomatoes

- ☐ 6 Bosc pears
- ☐ 3 lemons
- ☐ 1 orange
- ☐ ¾ cup parsley
- ☐ 1 cup loosely packed fresh mixed herbs, such as basil, chives, or parsley
- ☐ 1½ ounces microgreens

PANTRY & SPICES
- ☐ 2 (15-ounce) cans cannellini beans, drained
- ☐ 2 (15-ounce) cans chickpeas, drained
- ☐ ½ cup raw pumpkin seeds
- ☐ ½ cup walnuts
- ☐ Aleppo pepper, optional
- ☐ Harissa paste
- ☐ Garlic powder
- ☐ Salt
- ☐ Pepper
- ☐ Crushed red pepper
- ☐ ½ cup crushed pistachios plus more for serving

Butternut Squash Steak with Fennel-Potato Puree

Time to Make: 60 minutes (20 minutes inactive)

Serves: 4

WHY THIS RECIPE WORKS

Butternut squash is served two ways in this recipe. The neck of the squash is cut into steaks while the base of the squash is peeled and shaved into ribbons for a bright and fresh raw salad.

SUBSTITUTIONS

Butternut squash: Unpeeled acorn squash, cut into wedges
Asparagus: Edamame or quick-steamed sugar snap peas
Pistachios: Almonds, pecans, or walnut pieces

EQUIPMENT & LEFTOVERS

You'll need: Two baking sheets, food processor, and vegetable peeler
Leftovers: Store the butternut squash and the puree together in an airtight container in the fridge and enjoy within 3 days, and store the asparagus salad in a separate container in the fridge and enjoy within 3 days

INGREDIENTS

1 whole butternut squash

2 large fennel bulbs, cored and sliced into thin wedges

1½ pounds Yukon Gold potatoes, peeled and medium-diced

Salt and pepper to taste

2 tablespoons avocado oil, divided

1 head garlic, top cut off

1 pound asparagus, ribboned

2 tablespoons extra-virgin olive oil

½ cup crushed pistachios plus more for serving

½ cup loosely packed parsley, chopped

1 lemon, juiced

¾ cup plant-based Greek yogurt

2 tablespoons plant-based butter

Splash plant-based milk or water, if needed

(Continued on next page)

METHOD

1. **Preheat oven to 400°F.**

2. **Prepare the butternut squash:** Peel the whole butternut squash. Cut the neck from the bottom and keep separate. Cut the neck lengthwise into ¾-inch slices. One large squash should yield 6 slices. Set aside. Cut the bottom of the squash in half and scoop out the seeds. Use a vegetable peeler to shave the bottom of the squash into ribbons. Reserve the shaved squash for the salad.

3. **Roast the fennel and potatoes:** Arrange the fennel and potatoes on a baking sheet. Drizzle with 1 tablespoon avocado oil and sprinkle with salt and pepper. Wrap the garlic in foil to prevent it from burning. Transfer the fennel, potatoes, and garlic to the oven for 35 minutes until the potatoes are very tender and the garlic is very soft.

4. **Roast the butternut squash:** On a second baking sheet, arrange the squash "steaks" and drizzle with remaining avocado oil. Season with salt and pepper and transfer to the oven for 30 minutes, flipping once mid-way through. You may choose to broil the squash for 2 to 3 minutes at the end of cooking.

5. **As the vegetables roast, prepare the salad:** Combine the asparagus ribbons and squash ribbons in a bowl. Drizzle with the extra-virgin olive oil. Season with salt and pepper. Add the pistachios, parsley, and lemon juice and toss to combine. Season to taste. Transfer to the refrigerator until needed.

6. **Finish the puree:** Transfer the roasted fennel and potatoes to a food processor. Pop the garlic cloves out of their skins and add them to the processor. Add the Greek yogurt and butter and pulse until creamy. If needed, thin it out with a splash of plant-based milk or water until desired consistency is reached. Taste and season with salt and pepper.

7. **To serve:** Spoon the puree between shallow bowls and use the back of your spoon to smooth it into a circle. Place a squash steak on top and pile the shaved salad on top. Sprinkle with more pistachios. Enjoy!

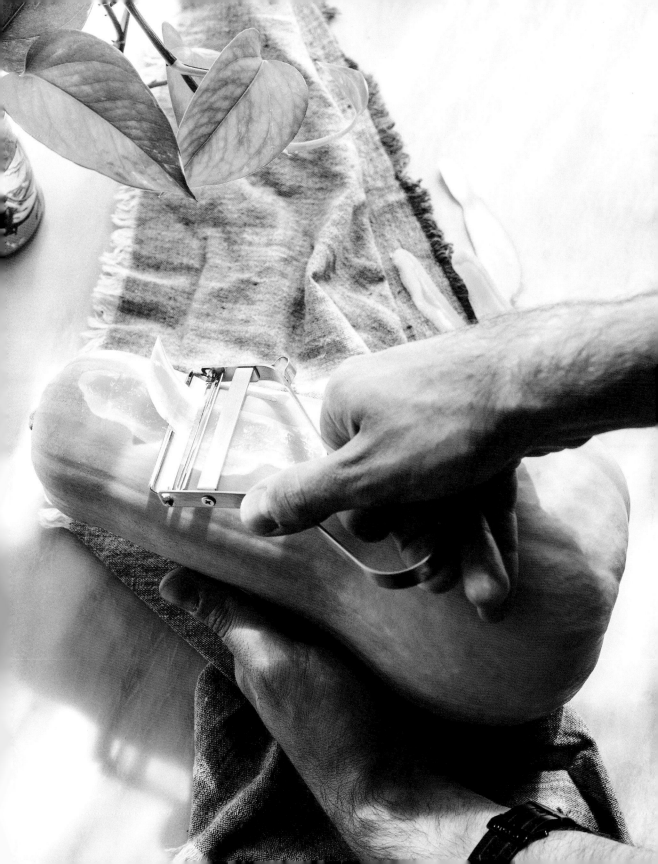

Farro and Burst Tomatoes in Celery Broth

Time to Make: 40 minutes

Serves: 4

WHY THIS RECIPE WORKS

Celery is the star of this delicious brothy farro. Be sure to use up those celery leaves, as they will add the most flavor to your broth. You will need 1 cup total mixed herbs, so use what is in season or use any of the leftover herbs in your crisper such as basil, parsley, chives, or even dill.

SUBSTITUTIONS

Farro: Your favorite rice or grain, such as brown rice, white rice, freekeh, or quinoa (cook time may vary)
Cherry tomatoes: 1 (15-ounce) can diced or whole peeled tomatoes

EQUIPMENT & LEFTOVERS

You'll need: Medium pot, wide pot, and colander
Leftovers: Store in an airtight container in the fridge for 3 days

INGREDIENTS

Salt, pepper, and crushed red pepper to taste

3 cups water

1 cup farro

2 teaspoons avocado oil

1 yellow onion, peeled and thinly sliced

4 ribs celery, diced, leaves torn

1 tablespoon plant-based butter, optional

1 pint cherry tomatoes

6 cups vegetable stock

1 cup loosely packed fresh mixed herbs, chopped

1 lemon, juiced

METHOD

1. **Cook the farro:** Bring the water to a boil in a medium pot and add salt. Add the farro, reduce heat, and simmer for 25 to 30 minutes until tender. Drain and rinse.

2. **Prepare the celery broth:** In a wide pot, heat the avocado oil over medium heat. Add the onion and cook until just beginning to soften, about 5 to 7 minutes. Add the celery with leaves and cook for 5 minutes until fragrant. Melt the plant-based butter into the pot (if using) until frothy. Season with salt and pepper and crushed red pepper. Add the cherry tomatoes and cook for 4 minutes until the skins just barely split open. Pour in the vegetable stock and bring to a boil. Reduce heat and simmer for 25 minutes. Season with salt and pepper to taste. Stir in the fresh mixed herbs and lemon juice and cook until bright green, about 2 to 3 minutes. Turn off the heat.

3. **To serve:** Divide the cooked farro between bowls and ladle the broth on top. Enjoy!

Pear Salad with White Beans and Vegetables

Time to Make: 25 minutes

Serves: 4

WHY THIS RECIPE WORKS

This salad is beautiful, bright, and filling and looks stunning served up on a large platter. It is endlessly versatile, so check out the substitutions below and mix and match ingredients depending on what's in season or what you have in your crisper!

SUBSTITUTIONS

Cannellini beans: Your favorite white bean, such as navy, great northern, or chickpeas
Baby spinach: Arugula or baby kale
Walnuts: Almonds, pistachios, cashews, or pumpkin seeds
Orange and lemon: Use interchangeably or try this recipe with lime or grapefruit
Bosc pears: Apples, figs, nectarines, or peaches
Asparagus: Your favorite crisp green vegetable, such as sugar snap peas, broccolini, or green beans

EQUIPMENT & LEFTOVERS

You'll need: Medium pot and colander
Leftovers: Store in an airtight container in the fridge for 3 days

INGREDIENTS

2 (15-ounce) cans cannellini beans, drained

3 ounces baby spinach

½ cup walnuts, lightly crushed

2 tablespoons extra-virgin olive oil, divided

1 orange, juiced and zested

Salt and pepper to taste

½ teaspoon Aleppo pepper or crushed red pepper plus more for serving, optional

2 Bosc pears, deseeded and thinly sliced lengthwise

1 lemon, juiced

3 ribs celery, thinly sliced, leaves torn

1 pound asparagus, woody ends trimmed

(Continued on next page)

METHOD

1. **Dress the beans:** In a bowl combine the beans, spinach, and walnuts. Drizzle with 1 tablespoon extra-virgin olive oil and add the orange juice and zest. Taste and season with salt and pepper. Add the Aleppo pepper or crushed red pepper (if using) and toss to coat. Set aside.

2. **Prepare the pears and celery:** In a second bowl add the pears and coat them with the lemon juice. Add the celery and drizzle with the remaining extra-virgin olive oil. Sprinkle lightly with salt and set aside.

3. **Cook the asparagus:** Bring a medium pot of water to a boil. Add the asparagus and cook for just 2 to 3 minutes until bright green. Do not overcook the asparagus! Drain and immediately cover with ice in the colander. Allow to cool for 5 minutes until the asparagus cools down.

4. **To serve:** Arrange the dressed beans, spinach, and walnuts on a serving platter and arrange the pears and celery on top. Arrange half the asparagus on one side of the platter and half on the opposite side. Sprinkle with black pepper and more Aleppo pepper, if desired. Enjoy!

Fennel Barley Stew with Celery

Time to Make: 60 minutes (20 minutes inactive)

Serves: 4

WHY THIS RECIPE WORKS

This barley stew is comforting enough to warm you up on a chilly day but not so heavy that it can't be enjoyed during warmer months. If you can find beet microgreens, they add a nice earthiness to the garnish, but a fresh, seasonal herb will brighten up the dish just as well.

SUBSTITUTIONS

Carrots: Golden beets, parsnips, or turnips
Pearl barley: Farro or brown rice (cook time may vary)
Microgreens: Fresh herbs like parsley or tarragon
Pumpkin seeds: Slivered almonds or chopped walnuts

EQUIPMENT & LEFTOVERS

You'll need: Wide pot and skillet
Leftovers: Store in an airtight container in the fridge for 3 days

INGREDIENTS

3 teaspoons avocado oil, divided

1 yellow onion, peeled and diced

4 carrots, peeled and small-diced

3 ribs celery, diced

1 fennel bulb, cored and sliced into thin wedges, fronds reserved for garnish

2 teaspoons garlic powder

½ teaspoon crushed red pepper

Salt and pepper to taste

1 cup pearl barley

6 cups vegetable stock

1 pint cherry tomatoes

½ cup raw pumpkin seeds

1½ ounces microgreens

1 teaspoon extra-virgin olive oil

METHOD

1. **Prepare the stew:** Heat 2 teaspoons avocado oil in a wide pot over medium heat. Add the onion and cook for 5 to 6 minutes until it just begins to soften. Add the carrots, celery, and fennel and cook for 10 minutes more until they begin to soften and turn golden brown around the edges. Add the garlic powder and crushed red pepper and cook for 45 seconds. Season all the aromatics with salt and pepper. Add the pearl barley and cook for 2 minutes.

2. **Simmer the stew:** Pour in the vegetable stock and bring to a boil. Reduce heat, cover, and simmer for 35 to 40 minutes or until the barley is tender. Taste and season to your preferences. Turn off the heat.

3. **Prepare the garnish:** Heat the remaining avocado oil in a skillet over high heat. Add the cherry tomatoes and cook until they begin to char, about 5 minutes. Transfer them to a bowl. Wipe out the skillet and return the heat to medium. Add the pumpkin seeds and cook for 1 minute until toasted. Transfer them to the bowl with the tomatoes. Season the tomatoes and pumpkin seeds with salt. Add the microgreens and a few pinches of fennel fronds. Drizzle with the extra-virgin olive oil and toss to coat. Set aside.

4. **To serve:** Divide the barley stew between bowls and serve with the pumpkin seed garnish on top. Enjoy!

Charred Pears with Harissa Chickpeas

Time to Make: 60 minutes (20 minutes inactive)

Serves: 4

WHY THIS RECIPE WORKS

A simple harissa broth with chickpeas gets upgraded in this recipe with the addition of beautifully charred pears. Make these Charred Pears with Harissa Chickpeas later in the week so that your pears have time to ripen. You can use firmer, slightly underripe pears but ripe pears will develop a much better char.

SUBSTITUTIONS

Bosc pears: Your favorite pear variety or nectarines or peaches
Harissa paste: Create a similar spice blend using the following ingredients: 2 teaspoons chili powder, 1 teaspoon paprika, 1 teaspoon smoked paprika, 1 teaspoon garlic powder, ½ teaspoon cayenne powder, and ½ teaspoon cumin powder

EQUIPMENT & LEFTOVERS

You'll need: Wide skillet
Leftovers: Store in an airtight container in the fridge for 3 days

INGREDIENTS

1 tablespoon avocado oil
4 Bosc pears, quartered and deseeded
Salt and pepper to taste
1 yellow onion, peeled and sliced into half-moons
1 tablespoon plant-based butter, optional
1–2 tablespoons harissa paste
2 cups vegetable stock
2 (15-ounce) cans chickpeas, drained
3 ounces baby spinach
¼ cup minced parsley, minced cilantro, or fresh
  microgreens for garnish

METHOD

1. **Cook the pears:** Heat the oil in a wide skillet over medium-high heat. Add the pears in batches, cut-side down, and cook without moving for 4 minutes. Turn the pears onto the other cut side and cook until it chars, an additional 3 to 4 minutes. You don't need to cook the skin side of the pear. If your pears aren't very ripe, you'll want to cook them a little longer to allow them to soften, but very ripe pears don't need to cook long. Transfer the charred pears to a plate and sprinkle with salt.

2. **Prepare the harissa chickpeas:** Add the onion to the same skillet and cook for 8 to 10 minutes until it begins to soften. Season with salt and pepper. Melt the plant-based butter (if using) into the onion. Once frothy, add the harissa paste and cook for 1 minute until fragrant. Pour in the vegetable stock and bring to a boil. Add the chickpeas. Reduce heat to medium-low and cook until the broth has reduced slightly and the onions have softened, about 15 minutes. If the liquid reduces too much, add a bit more stock or water. Taste and season with salt and pepper. Stir in the spinach and cook for 5 minutes until wilted. Turn off the heat.

3. **To serve:** Ladle the chickpeas between bowls and arrange the charred pear on top. Garnish with fresh herbs or microgreens. Enjoy!

PLAN 2: WEEK 4

This recipe plan includes dinner recipes for five days, all of which serve four. To conquer the grocery store in one shopping trip, the next page outlines a detailed grocery list, with items separated by store department. You will also find storage, freezing, and thawing tips to help you plan your week. This plan is all about simple dressings and sauces. Pay special attention to the key players throughout the week (green beans and shitake mushrooms) and be sure to buy the freshest and healthiest of those ingredients that you can find because you will use them for multiple recipes.

THE MENU

MONDAY
Sichuan Soba Bowls

TUESDAY
Salad with Orange-Maple Vinaigrette

WEDNESDAY
Radish Top Miso Ramen

THURSDAY
Roasted Vegetable Couscous with
Strawberry Salad

FRIDAY
Pasta with Basil-Mint Gremolata

PLAN 2: WEEK 4
CONQUERING THE GROCERY STORE

FOOD SAFETY GUIDELINES

Buying groceries for the entire week can require some forethought, so be sure to refer to the FDA's storage and freezing guidelines for your ingredients. To keep herbs and leafy greens fresh through the week, wrap them in a damp paper towel and store in a bag in your crisper. Refresh the paper towel periodically through the week to keep them extra fresh.

GRAINS
- ☐ 1 cup couscous

OIL
- ☐ Avocado oil
- ☐ Extra-virgin olive oil

PLANT-BASED DAIRY
- ☐ 8 ounces plant-based Greek yogurt

STOCK
- ☐ 4 cups vegetable stock

FRUITS & VEGETABLES
- ☐ 2 yellow onions
- ☐ 8 cloves garlic
- ☐ 1 (1-inch) piece ginger
- ☐ 1 jalapeño pepper
- ☐ 1 Thai chili pepper, optional
- ☐ 1 red Fresno chili pepper
- ☐ 18 ounces shitake mushrooms
- ☐ 1 pound sweet potatoes
- ☐ 1 head cauliflower
- ☐ 24 ounces green beans
- ☐ 12 ounces Brussels sprouts
- ☐ 1 bunch red radishes with leafy greens
- ☐ 5 ounces baby spinach
- ☐ 4 small heads little gem lettuce
- ☐ 1 pint cherry tomatoes
- ☐ 8 ounces pomegranate seeds
- ☐ 3 lemons
- ☐ 1 blood orange
- ☐ 1 lime
- ☐ 1 pint strawberries
- ☐ 4 scallions
- ☐ 1 cup parsley
- ☐ ½ cup loosely packed basil leaves
- ☐ ½ ounce mint
- ☐ 1 small bunch dill
- ☐ ½ ounce edible flowers, optional
- ☐ 2 avocados

(Continued on next page)

PANTRY & SPICES

- ☐ 16 ounces soba noodles
- ☐ 16 ounces fresh or frozen ramen noodles
- ☐ 16 ounces medium shells
- ☐ 1 cup chopped walnuts
- ☐ Maple syrup
- ☐ White wine vinegar
- ☐ Spicy Dijon mustard
- ☐ Red miso paste
- ☐ Tahini
- ☐ Chili oil
- ☐ Sesame oil
- ☐ Soy sauce
- ☐ Mirin
- ☐ Sichuan peppercorns
- ☐ Black or white sesame seeds
- ☐ Star anise pods
- ☐ Shichimi-togarashi
- ☐ Chili powder
- ☐ Cumin powder
- ☐ Paprika
- ☐ Cayenne powder
- ☐ Salt
- ☐ Flaky sea salt
- ☐ Pepper
- ☐ White pepper, optional
- ☐ Crushed red pepper

Sichuan Soba Bowls

Time to Make: 35 minutes

Serves: 4

WHY THIS RECIPE WORKS

Mouthwatering homemade Sichuan oil, earthy shitake mushrooms, and tender-crisp green beans make for a flavorful Monday night dinner.

SUBSTITUTIONS

Thai chili peppers: Your favorite hot pepper, such as habanero, jalapeño, or serrano pepper
Shitake mushrooms: Any mushroom variety, such as cremini, baby bella, oyster, or maitake
Baby spinach: Baby kale or chopped dandelion greens
Soba noodles: Udon or ramen noodles

EQUIPMENT & LEFTOVERS

You'll need: Small pot, wok (or wide pot), large pot, colander
Leftovers: Store the Sichuan Soba Bowls in an airtight container in the fridge for 3 days, and store the homemade Sichuan chili oil in an airtight jar in the fridge for 7 days

INGREDIENTS

½ cup + 3 teaspoons avocado oil

1 Thai chili pepper, minced, optional

5 cloves garlic, peeled and minced

1 tablespoon Sichuan peppercorns, crushed

3 star anise pods

2 teaspoons chili oil

2 teaspoons sesame oil

1 (1-inch) piece ginger, peeled and minced

Salt and pepper to taste

16 ounces soba noodles

1 yellow onion, peeled and thinly sliced into half-moons

10 ounces shitake mushrooms

12 ounces green beans, halved crosswise

1 tablespoon soy sauce

5 ounces baby spinach

(Continued on page 123)

METHOD

1. **Prepare the Sichuan oil:** In a small pot combine ½ cup avocado oil, the Thai chili pepper, garlic, Sichuan peppercorns, star anise, chili oil, sesame oil, and ginger. Turn the heat to medium. Once the oil begins to bubble, reduce the heat to low and simmer for 25 minutes. Season with salt.

2. **Boil the soba noodles:** Meanwhile, bring a large pot of salted water to a boil. Cook the soba according to package instructions. Drain and rinse and set aside.

3. **Prepare the vegetables:** Heat 1 teaspoon avocado oil in a wok over medium-high heat. Once it begins to shimmer, add the onion and cook, stirring often, for 8 minutes until it begins to soften and turn golden brown. Adjust the heat as necessary to prevent it from burning. Add remaining avocado oil and the shitake mushrooms and cook for an additional 6 to 8 minutes until the mushrooms crisp up around the edges. Season with salt and pepper. Add the green beans to the wok and cook for 3 minutes. Add the soy sauce to the vegetables and stir to coat. Cook for 2 minutes or until the green beans are bright green and tender-crisp. Taste and season with salt and pepper, if needed. Add the baby spinach to the wok.

4. **As soon as the baby spinach begins to wilt, add the cooked soba noodles to the wok:** Toss to combine the noodles until they warm up. Pour half the Sichuan oil over the noodles and toss to coat. Cook for 1 minute more over medium heat. Turn the heat off.

5. **To serve:** Divide the cooked soba noodles between bowls. Serve with more Sichuan oil on the side. Enjoy!

Salad with Orange-Maple Vinaigrette

Time to Make: 20 minutes

Serves: 4

WHY THIS RECIPE WORKS

A few simple ingredients come together to make this beautiful all-season salad. If you can't find edible flowers, add your favorite crisp, seasonal ingredient, such as cucumber or shaved asparagus.

SUBSTITUTIONS

Little gem lettuce: 2 heads romaine lettuce or 5 ounces baby spinach
Walnuts: Your favorite nut variety, such as cashews, pecans, or slivered almonds
Avocados: If you can't find a good avocado, replace it with a vegetable like asparagus, sugar snap peas, or broccolini
Pomegranate seeds: Halved red, seedless grapes or halved figs

EQUIPMENT & LEFTOVERS

You'll need: Mixing bowls and whisk
Leftovers: Store in an airtight container in the fridge for 3 days

INGREDIENTS

2 avocados

1 lemon, juiced

4 small heads little gem lettuce, large leaves torn in half and small leaves kept whole

1 cup chopped walnuts

8 ounces pomegranate seeds

1 tablespoon + ½ cup extra-virgin olive oil, divided

½ ounce edible flowers, optional

Salt and pepper to taste

1 blood orange, juiced and zested

2 tablespoons maple syrup

1 teaspoon white wine vinegar

1 teaspoon spicy Dijon mustard

Pinch crushed red pepper

Pinch flaky sea salt

Pinch freshly ground black pepper

(Continued on page 126)

METHOD

1. **Prepare the avocados:** Peel the avocados and halve them lengthwise, around the pit. Remove the seed and discard it. Slice each half of the avocado crosswise into thin slices and sprinkle half the lemon juice over the avocados. Set aside.

2. **Dress the salad:** Combine the lettuce, walnuts, pomegranate seeds, 1 tablespoon extra-virgin olive oil, and the remaining lemon juice in a large bowl and toss to combine. Add the edible flowers and a sprinkle of salt and pepper and gently toss to incorporate the flowers throughout the salad. Set aside.

3. **Prepare the vinaigrette:** In a bowl, combine the blood orange juice and zest, maple syrup, white wine vinegar, mustard, crushed red pepper, flaky sea salt, and freshly ground black pepper and whisk until combined. Taste and season to your preferences. Whisking continuously, slowly pour in the remaining extra-virgin olive oil until it is completely emulsified. Taste and season to your preferences.

4. **Finish the salad:** Pour half the vinaigrette over the salad and gently toss to coat.

5. **To serve:** Divide the salad between bowls. Arrange an avocado half on top of each salad and drizzle more vinaigrette on top. Enjoy!

Radish Top Miso Ramen

Time to Make: 50 minutes (20 minutes inactive)

Serves: 4

WHY THIS RECIPE WORKS

Don't throw away those radish greens! I use radish greens both on and in this Radish Top Miso Ramen for an earthy element that pairs perfectly with creamy ramen. Tahini and miso create a dreamy combination in this comforting broth that will leave you wanting ramen every day.

SUBSTITUTIONS

Shitake mushrooms: Any mushroom variety, such as cremini, baby bella, oyster, or maitake
Shichimi-togarashi: If you cannot find shichimi-togarashi, use a bit of crushed red pepper instead
Red miso: White miso
Ramen noodles: Soba or udon

EQUIPMENT & LEFTOVERS

You'll need: Large pot, medium pot, colander
Leftovers: Store the broth and the ramen noodles separately in airtight containers in the fridge for up to 3 days, and store the dressed radishes separately in an airtight container in the fridge for up to 2 days

INGREDIENTS

1 tablespoon avocado oil

1 yellow onion, peeled and thinly sliced

8 ounces shitake mushrooms, thinly sliced

¼ cup mirin

1 tablespoon soy sauce

4 cups vegetable stock

1 bunch red radishes

2 teaspoons sesame oil

2 teaspoons shichimi-togarashi

Salt and pepper to taste

1 teaspoon black or white sesame seeds

2 tablespoons red miso paste

⅓ cup tahini

2 tablespoons chili oil to taste

16 ounces fresh or frozen ramen noodles

12 ounces fresh green beans, halved crosswise

(Continued on page 129)

METHOD

1. **Prepare the broth:** Heat the avocado oil in a large pot over medium heat. Add the onions and cook, stirring regularly, for 5 minutes until they just begin to soften. Add the sliced shitake mushrooms to the onions and cook for 5 to 6 minutes. Season with salt and pepper. Add the mirin and soy sauce to the mushrooms. Pour in the vegetable stock and bring to a boil. Reduce heat and simmer for 30 minutes.

2. **Prepare the radishes:** Cut the radish greens from the radishes. Rinse the radish greens thoroughly and reserve for later. Scrub the radishes and thinly slice them into rounds. In a bowl combine the sliced radishes with sesame oil, shichimi-togarashi, salt, and sesame seeds and set aside.

3. **Prepare the miso mixture:** In a separate bowl combine the miso paste, tahini, and chili oil and whisk until mostly smooth. Set aside.

4. **Cook the noodles:** Right before the broth finishes simmering, add the noodles to a large pot of boiling water. Drain and divide the cooked noodles between four bowls.

5. **Finish the ramen broth:** Turn the heat down to very low on the broth. Whisk in the miso mixture. Add the green beans and reserved radish greens and allow the heat from the broth to cook the beans. Once the beans are bright green and tender-crisp, turn off the heat. Taste and season to your preferences.

6. **To serve:** Ladle the hot broth over the ramen noodles. Arrange the sliced, dressed radishes on top. Enjoy!

Roasted Vegetable Couscous
with Strawberry Salad

Time to Make: 50 minutes

Serves: 4

WHY THIS RECIPE WORKS

Roasted vegetables paired with fluffy couscous and a plant-based dill yogurt taste great on their own, but add a bright and spicy strawberry salsa on top and you'll be completely infatuated with this gorgeous, easy dinner.

SUBSTITUTIONS

Cauliflower: Green cabbage cut into steaks
Brussels sprouts: Broccoli florets
Sweet potatoes: Yukon Gold potato or butternut squash cubes
Couscous: Your favorite grain or small pasta, such as farro, pearl couscous, or pearl barley (cook time will vary)
Strawberries: If strawberries aren't in season, try cherries, diced nectarines, tomatoes, mango, or even peaches

EQUIPMENT & LEFTOVERS

You'll need: Baking sheet, Microplane, and medium pot
Leftovers: Store in an airtight container in the fridge for 3 days

INGREDIENTS

2 tablespoons chili powder

2 tablespoons cumin powder

2 teaspoons paprika

½ teaspoon cayenne powder, optional

¼ teaspoon white pepper, optional

1 pound sweet potatoes, peeled and sliced into half-moons

1 head of cauliflower, sliced into 4 steaks

2 tablespoons avocado oil, divided

Salt and pepper to taste

12 ounces Brussels sprouts, halved

8 ounces plant-based Greek yogurt

½ cup loosely packed parsley, minced

1 small bunch of dill, minced

2 lemons, juiced and zested

1 pint strawberries, thinly sliced

4 scallions, minced

1 jalapeño, minced

1¼ cups water or vegetable stock

1 teaspoon extra-virgin olive oil, plus more for garnish

1 cup couscous

(Continued on page 132)

METHOD

1. **Preheat oven to 425°F.**

2. **Make the spice mixture:** Combine the chili powder, cumin powder, paprika, cayenne powder, and white pepper (if using) in a bowl and stir to combine. Set aside.

3. **Roast the vegetables:** Arrange sweet potatoes and cauliflower steaks on a baking sheet. Drizzle with 1 tablespoon avocado oil and sprinkle half the spice mixture on top. Season with salt and pepper. Transfer to the oven for 15 minutes. Combine the Brussels sprouts with remaining avocado oil and the rest of the spice mixture. Season with salt and pepper. After the cauliflower has roasted, remove the baking sheet from the oven, flip the cauliflower and sweet potatoes, and arrange the seasoned Brussels sprouts on top. Return to the oven for an additional 15 to 20 minutes until the Brussels sprouts are cooked through and the cauliflower begins to char. Turn off the heat and leave the vegetables in the warm oven as you finish the recipe.

4. **Prepare the yogurt:** Combine the Greek yogurt, parsley, dill, and lemon juice and zest in a bowl and whisk until smooth. Refrigerate until needed.

5. **Prepare the strawberry salad:** In a bowl combine the strawberries, scallions, jalapeño, and juice and zest from 1 lemon. Season with a touch of salt and pepper. Refrigerate until needed.

6. **Once the vegetables have nearly finished roasting, prepare the couscous:** In a medium pot, combine the water or stock, salt, and extra-virgin olive oil. Bring to a boil, then pour in the couscous. Stir to combine, then remove pot from the heat. Cover and let stand for 5 minutes. After the couscous has steamed, remove the lid and fluff with a fork. Taste and season again to your preferences.

7. **Finish the roasted vegetable couscous:** In a large bowl, combine the cooked couscous, sweet potatoes, and Brussels sprouts.

8. **To serve:** Spoon the yogurt onto plates and smooth it out with the back of your spoon. Pile the couscous on top. Place a cauliflower steak on top of the couscous and spoon the strawberry salsa on top. Finish each dish with a drizzle of extra-virgin olive oil, if desired. Enjoy!

Pasta with Basil-Mint Gremolata

Time to Make: 25 minutes

Serves: 4

WHY THIS RECIPE WORKS

This easy recipe is a great way to finish off any leftover herbs you have from this week's meal plan. For the gremolata, I use basil and mint, but feel free to throw in a little dill, parsley, minced scallions, or whatever else you have on hand. You'll want about 1 cup of loosely packed herbs total. If you want to stretch this meal even further, add a can of drained chickpeas with the tomatoes and red Fresno chili pepper and continue with the recipe as is.

SUBSTITUTIONS

Medium shells: Any pasta will do, but try to use a shape that catches the sauce well such as penne or rigatoni
Red Fresno chili pepper: Your favorite hot pepper, such as habanero, jalapeño, or serrano pepper, or crushed red pepper to taste
Lime: Lemon

EQUIPMENT & LEFTOVERS

You'll need: Large pot, Microplane, food processor, and colander
Leftovers: Store in an airtight container in the fridge for 3 days

INGREDIENTS

16 ounces medium shells

½ cup parsley, minced

½ cup loosely packed basil leaves, minced

½ ounce mint, minced, plus more for garnish

3 cloves garlic, minced

1 lime, juiced and zested

½ cup extra-virgin olive oil plus more as needed

1 pint cherry tomatoes, quartered

1 red Fresno chili pepper, thinly sliced

Salt and pepper to taste

METHOD

1. **Cook the pasta:** Bring a large pot of salted water to a boil. Cook pasta until al dente. Drain and set aside.

2. **Prepare the gremolata:** Combine the parsley, basil, mint, garlic, lime juice, lime zest, and extra-virgin olive oil in a food processor and pulse until finely chopped. If the gremolata is too thick, add a touch more extra-virgin olive oil. Transfer to a bowl.

3. **Finish the pasta:** In a large bowl, add the cherry tomatoes and the red Fresno chili pepper. Season with salt and pepper. Add half the gremolata to the tomatoes and toss to coat. Add the warm pasta and toss to combine.

4. **To serve:** Divide pasta between bowls and garnish with the rest of the gremolata and mint leaves, if desired.

PLAN 3: WEEK 1

This recipe plan includes dinner recipes for five days, all of which serve four. To conquer the grocery store in one shopping trip, the next page outlines a detailed grocery list, with items separated by store department. You will also find storage, freezing, and thawing tips to help you plan your week. This plan is all about tangy, bright, and slightly acidic flavors. Pay special attention to the key players throughout the week (zucchini, tomatillo peppers, and plantains) and be sure to buy the freshest and healthiest of those ingredients that you can find, because you will use them for multiple recipes.

THE MENU

MONDAY
Warm Farro Salad with Charred Zucchini

TUESDAY
Brothy White Beans with Radicchio

WEDNESDAY
Quinoa Plantain Bowl

THURSDAY
Kale Soup with Lime-Cilantro Chickpeas

FRIDAY
Black Bean Burgers with Tomatillo Salsa

PLAN 3: WEEK 1
CONQUERING THE GROCERY STORE

FOOD SAFETY GUIDELINES

Buying groceries for the entire week can require some forethought, so be sure to refer to the FDA's storage and freezing guidelines for your ingredients. To keep herbs and leafy greens fresh through the week, wrap them in a damp paper towel and store in a bag in your crisper. Refresh the paper towel periodically through the week to keep them extra fresh.

GRAINS

☐ 1 cup farro

☐ 1 cup quinoa

OIL

☐ Avocado oil

☐ Extra-virgin olive oil

PLANT-BASED DAIRY

☐ 2 tablespoons plant-based butter

STOCK

☐ 10 cups vegetable stock

FRUITS & VEGETABLES

☐ 4 yellow onions

☐ 1 shallot

☐ 2 heads garlic

☐ ½ pound mixed mushrooms, such as shitake and cremini

☐ 1 pound (2 whole) sweet potatoes

☐ 2 medium zucchini

☐ 1½ pounds tomatillos

☐ 1 red Fresno chili pepper

☐ 4 jalapeño peppers

☐ 1 pound curly kale

☐ 1 small head red cabbage

☐ 1 head radicchio

☐ 4 ounces watercress

☐ 2 large, ripe plantains

☐ 4 medium yellow plantains, slightly ripe but not completely black

☐ 2 lemons

☐ 7 limes

☐ ½ cup dill

☐ ½ cup parsley

☐ ¾ cup cilantro

☐ 2 ounces basil

☐ 1 avocado

(Continued on next page)

PANTRY & SPICES

- ☐ 2 (15-ounce) cans butter beans
- ☐ 2 (15-ounce) cans chickpeas
- ☐ 2 (15-ounce) cans black beans
- ☐ 2 (7-ounce) cans hot green chili peppers, optional
- ☐ 6 ounces green olives
- ☐ Vegan mayonnaise
- ☐ Cassava or all-purpose flour
- ☐ Tahini
- ☐ Brown sugar

- ☐ Chili powder
- ☐ Chipotle powder
- ☐ Smoked paprika
- ☐ Paprika
- ☐ Cumin powder
- ☐ Cayenne powder
- ☐ Salt
- ☐ Pepper
- ☐ Crushed red pepper

Warm Farro Salad with Charred Zucchini

Time to Make: 35 minutes

Serves: 4

WHY THIS RECIPE WORKS

This Warm Farro Salad with Charred Zucchini is aromatic and easy to make, and who doesn't love a filling salad recipe? Load up this warm farro with charred zucchini, green olives, and plenty of basil and fresh watercress for a sweetly savory dinner.

SUBSTITUTIONS

Farro: Your favorite rice or grain, such as brown rice, white rice, freekeh, or quinoa (cook time will vary)
Red Fresno chili pepper: Your favorite hot pepper, such as habanero, jalapeño, or serrano pepper, or crushed red pepper to taste
Watercress: Your favorite microgreen or baby spinach, arugula, or baby kale

EQUIPMENT & LEFTOVERS

You'll need: Medium pot and large, ovenproof skillet
Leftovers: Store in an airtight container in the fridge for 3 days

INGREDIENTS

3 cups water
Salt and pepper to taste
1 cup farro
4 teaspoons avocado oil, divided
1 tablespoon plant-based butter
1 yellow onion, peeled and diced
2 medium zucchini, sliced into half-moons
1 red Fresno chili pepper, sliced into rounds
2 ounces basil leaves, cut into fine chiffonade, plus a few leaves reserved for garnish
6 ounces green olives, if desired
4 ounces watercress

METHOD

1. **Cook the farro:** Bring 3 cups of salted water to a boil in a medium pot. Add the farro, reduce heat, and simmer for 25 to 30 minutes until tender. Drain and rinse.

2. **Sauté the onions:** Heat 2 teaspoons of the avocado oil in a wide skillet over medium heat. Add the plant-based butter, and once frothy, add the onions. Cook the onions, stirring often, for 12 minutes until the onions begin to turn golden brown. They do not need to be fully caramelized. Season lightly with salt.

3. **Broil the zucchini:** Turn on the broiler. In the same skillet used for the onions, arrange the zucchini and sliced red Fresno chili pepper on top of the onions in an even layer. It's okay if there is some overlap. Drizzle with the remaining avocado oil and season with salt and pepper. Transfer the skillet to the broiler and cook, regularly checking, for 3 to 5 minutes until char marks develop on the zucchini. It may take longer depending on your broiler but check the zucchini often!

(Continued on page 141)

4. **Finish the vegetables:** Transfer the skillet back to the stovetop and turn the heat to medium-high. Allow the zucchini to cook without moving for an additional 5 minutes or until excess water is cooked off and the zucchini bottoms begin to brown. Don't overcook the zucchini! It should still be bright green in places. Carefully add the chiffonade of basil to the skillet along with the olives and watercress and toss to combine. Taste and season with salt and pepper and cook for 1 to 2 minutes until the watercress wilts.

5. **To serve:** Add the cooked farro to the skillet and toss to combine. Taste and season again to your preferences. Turn off the heat and serve warm. Garnish with a few additional basil leaves, if desired.

Brothy White Beans with Radicchio

Time to Make: 40 minutes (20 minutes inactive)

Serves: 4

WHY THIS RECIPE WORKS

Radicchio is a beautifully bitter vegetable that pairs perfectly with these herby, creamy beans. Although it may look like cabbage, radicchio is part of the chicory family, along with escarole and curly endives. In this recipe, bitter radicchio gets a little massage first and marinates with extra-virgin olive oil, lemon juice, and salt to calm the bitter flavors. If you do not have fresh dill or fresh parsley, simply swap in their dry counterparts.

SUBSTITUTIONS

Radicchio: Belgian endives or escarole
Butter beans: Your favorite white bean, such as cannellini, great northern, navy beans, or chickpeas

EQUIPMENT & LEFTOVERS

You'll need: Wide pot, Microplane, and food processor
Leftovers: Store in an airtight container in the fridge for 3 days

INGREDIENTS

2 lemons, juiced and zested

1–2 tablespoons extra-virgin olive oil

1 head radicchio, leaves separated

Pinch flaky salt to taste

2 teaspoons avocado oil

1 yellow onion, peeled and diced

6 cloves garlic, peeled

½ teaspoon crushed red pepper to taste

4 cups vegetable stock

2 (15-ounce) cans butter beans, drained

Salt and pepper to taste

1 tablespoon plant-based butter or tahini, to thicken the broth

½ cup loosely packed fresh dill leaves or 1 tablespoon dried dill

½ cup loosely packed fresh parsley leaves or 1 tablespoon dried parsley

(Continued on page 144)

METHOD

1. **Marinate the radicchio:** In a bowl combine the juice and zest of 1 lemon and extra-virgin olive oil. Add the radicchio and use your hands to massage the marinade into the leaves. Season with flaky salt and set aside for 30 minutes.

2. **Prepare the brothy white beans:** Heat the avocado oil in a wide pot over medium-high heat. Add the onion and cook for 8 to 10 minutes, stirring regularly, until it is completely softened and just beginning to brown. Place the garlic in a food processor and pulse until minced. (Note: You will use the food processor again for the dill and parsley, but you do not need to clean it out!) Add the garlic to the pot. Add in the crushed red pepper and cook for 45 seconds until it is fragrant. Add the vegetable stock and bring to a boil. Add the beans. Reduce heat and simmer for 30 minutes until the broth is reduced and thickened slightly. Season the broth with salt and pepper to taste. Note: Add 1 tablespoon of plant-based butter or tahini to help thicken the broth. Meanwhile, place the dill and parsley in the food processor and pulse until minced.

3. **Finish the beans:** Stir in the juice and zest from the remaining lemon and the minced dill and parsley and season the broth again to taste. Cook for 4 to 5 minutes until the herbs are bright green. Turn off the heat.

4. **To serve:** Arrange a few marinated radicchio leaves in a shallow bowl and ladle the beans on top. Enjoy!

Quinoa Plantain Bowl

Time to Make: 45 minutes

Serves: 4

WHY THIS RECIPE WORKS

Cooked quinoa is paired with all the best things in this recipe: stewed black beans, a crisp, spicy cabbage slaw, and roasted plantains and sweet potatoes. Use ripe plantains to add a delicious sweetness to this flavorful quinoa bowl.

SUBSTITUTIONS

Quinoa: Freekeh or white rice (cook time will vary)

EQUIPMENT & LEFTOVERS

You'll need: Two small pots and two baking sheets
Leftovers: Store in an airtight container in the fridge for 3 days

INGREDIENTS

2 cups water

1 cup quinoa

Salt and pepper to taste

1 pound (2 whole) sweet potatoes, peeled and small-diced

3 tablespoons + 2 teaspoons avocado oil, divided

1 tablespoon + 2 teaspoons chili powder, divided

1 tablespoon + 1 teaspoon cumin powder, divided

2 large, ripe plantains, peeled and cut into rounds

1 yellow onion, peeled and cut into thin wedges

1 (15-ounce) can black beans, drained

1 cup vegetable stock

½ cup vegan mayonnaise

½ cup loosely packed cilantro leaves, minced

3 limes, divided

1 small head red cabbage, cored and thinly sliced

1 jalapeño, thinly sliced into rounds

METHOD

1. **Preheat oven to 400°F.**

2. **Cook the quinoa:** Bring the water to a boil in a small pot. Pour in the quinoa and reduce heat to a simmer. Cover and allow the quinoa to simmer for 15 minutes or until the water is absorbed. Turn off the heat and let it stand for 10 minutes. Fluff with a fork and season with salt.

3. **Roast the sweet potatoes and plantains:** Arrange the sweet potatoes on one baking sheet and drizzle with 1 tablespoon avocado oil. Season with 1 tablespoon chili powder, 1 tablespoon cumin powder, salt, and pepper and toss to coat evenly. On a second baking sheet, arrange the plantains in an even layer and drizzle with 2 tablespoons avocado oil. Season with salt. Transfer both of the baking sheets to the oven and roast for 15 minutes. Flip both the sweet potatoes and the plantains and roast an additional 15 to 20 minutes until well-browned all over. The sweet potatoes should be fork tender.

(Continued on page 147)

4. **Prepare the stewed black beans:** Heat 2 teaspoons avocado oil in a small pot over medium heat. Add the yellow onion and cook for 5 minutes until it begins to soften. Add 1 teaspoon chili powder and 1 teaspoon cumin powder and cook for 1 minute until fragrant. Add the black beans and cook for an additional 1 minute. Season with salt and pepper. Pour in the vegetable stock and bring to a boil. Simmer uncovered for 25 minutes, stirring occasionally. If the broth reduces too quickly, add a splash or two of water to loosen up the black beans.

5. **Prepare the cabbage slaw:** In a large bowl, combine the vegan mayonnaise, remaining chili powder, cilantro leaves, and juice and zest from 2 limes. Season to taste with salt and pepper. Add the cabbage and jalapeño to the bowl of dressing and toss to coat. Refrigerate until needed.

6. **To serve:** Divide the cooked quinoa between bowls. Arrange the roasted sweet potatoes and plantains on top. Spoon the black beans and cabbage slaw on each dish. Serve with lime wedges. Enjoy!

Kale Soup with Lime-Cilantro Chickpeas

Time to Make: 45 minutes

Serves: 4

WHY THIS RECIPE WORKS

An easy recipe with just ten ingredients—is it too good to be true? Not in this Kale Soup with Lime-Cilantro Chickpeas. Rather than cook the chickpeas into the broth, we marinate them in lime juice and zest, then pile them on top of the soup for a bright and herby finish.

SUBSTITUTIONS

Tomatillos: Green tomatoes or red bell peppers
Kale: Spinach or Swiss chard
Lime: Lemon

EQUIPMENT & LEFTOVERS

You'll need: Baking sheet, foil, large pot, Microplane, and immersion blender
Leftovers: Store in an airtight container in the fridge for 3 days

INGREDIENTS

1 pound tomatillos, husks removed

1–2 jalapeño peppers

2 tablespoons + 2 teaspoons avocado oil plus more as needed

1 head of garlic, top cut off

Salt and pepper to taste

1 yellow onion, peeled and sliced into wedges

1 (7-ounce) can hot green chili peppers, diced, optional

5 cups vegetable stock

2 (15-ounce) cans chickpeas, drained

2 limes, juiced and zested

1 tablespoon extra-virgin olive oil

¼ cup loosely packed cilantro leaves, roughly chopped

1 pound curly kale, chopped

2 tablespoons tahini, optional

(Continued on page 150)

METHOD

1. **Preheat oven to 400°F.**

2. **Char the tomatillos, jalapeños, and garlic:** Place tomatillos and jalapeño peppers on a baking sheet and drizzle with 1 tablespoon avocado oil. Drizzle the garlic with 1 tablespoon avocado oil and wrap the garlic in foil. Season the vegetables with salt. Transfer to the oven and roast for 15 to 20 minutes until they char.

3. **While the vegetables roast, prepare the kale soup:** Heat the remaining avocado oil in a large pot and add the onion. Cook for 8 to 10 minutes until it begins to brown around the edges. Add the hot green chili peppers and cook for 4 minutes. Season lightly with salt. Pour in the vegetable stock and bring to a boil. Reduce heat and simmer for 15 minutes.

4. **Prepare the lime-cilantro chickpeas:** In a bowl, combine the chickpeas, lime juice and zest, extra-virgin olive oil, and cilantro. Season lightly with salt. Set aside at room temperature until needed.

5. **Prepare the charred vegetables:** Carefully pop the garlic cloves from the skin. Trim the stems off the jalapeño peppers and remove any woody parts from the tops of the tomatillos.

6. **Finish cooking the soup:** Add the garlic cloves, jalapeños, and tomatillos to the soup. Add the kale and cook for an additional 15 minutes until the kale is bright green and tender. Taste and season with salt and pepper.

7. **Blend the soup:** Use an immersion blender to blend the soup until smooth. If you do not have an immersion blender, you can transfer the soup to a blender. Alternatively, blend the garlic, jalapeño, and tomatillos in a food processor before adding it to the soup and leave the rest of the soup unblended. If the soup seems a bit thin, add the tahini.

8. **To serve:** Ladle the blended soup into bowls and pile the lime-cilantro chickpeas on top. Enjoy!

Black Bean Burgers with Tomatillo Salsa

Time to Make: About 1 hour

Serves: 4

WHY THIS RECIPE WORKS

This recipe makes enough for four open-faced burgers. You can top the fried plantains with the burgers or make the plantains smaller and serve them as traditional burger buns.

SUBSTITUTIONS

Tomatillo peppers: If you cannot find tomatillo peppers, use fresh tomatoes instead
Shallot: Small yellow onion
Cassava flour: Arrowroot powder, tapioca flour, coconut flour, all-purpose flour, nut-based flour, or even yellow cornmeal

EQUIPMENT & LEFTOVERS

You'll need: Food processor, wide skillet, and paper towels
Leftovers: Store in an airtight container in the fridge for 3 days

INGREDIENTS

½ pound tomatillos, husks removed

1 shallot, peeled and thinly sliced

1 jalapeño, diced

1 avocado, peeled, diced, and pit removed

2 limes, juiced

Salt and pepper to taste

½ cup vegan mayonnaise

1 teaspoon + 1 tablespoon chili powder, divided

½ teaspoon chipotle powder

½ teaspoon smoked paprika

½ pound mixed mushrooms, such as shitake and cremini

2 tablespoons + 1–2 teaspoons avocado oil, divided

1 (7-ounce) can hot green chili peppers, optional

4 cloves garlic, peeled

1 (15-ounce) can black beans, drained

2 teaspoons cumin powder

2 teaspoons brown sugar

2 teaspoons paprika

Cayenne powder to taste, optional

4 slightly ripe but not completely black medium yellow plantains

4 tablespoons cassava flour, divided

(Continued on page 153)

METHOD

1. **Prepare the tomatillo salsa:** Combine the tomatillos, shallot, jalapeño, avocado, and juice from 1 lime in a bowl. Season with salt and pepper and transfer to the refrigerator until needed.

2. **Prepare the chipotle mayonnaise:** In a separate bowl combine the mayonnaise, 1 teaspoon chili powder, the chipotle powder, and smoked paprika and whisk until smooth. If the mayonnaise seems too thick, add a splash of water to thin it out. Taste and season with salt and pepper.

3. **Prepare the black bean burgers:** Add the mushrooms to a food processor and pulse until finely chopped. Heat 1 tablespoon avocado oil in a wide skillet over medium-high heat. Once hot, add the minced mushrooms and cook them for 8 to 10 minutes until they release water and the water begins to evaporate. Season with salt and pepper. Add the chili peppers, garlic, and black beans to the food processor and pulse until finely chopped. It's okay if the black beans are a little lumpy. Add the mixture to the skillet with the mushrooms and cook for 4 more minutes. Season the mushrooms and beans with 1 tablespoon chili powder, the cumin powder, brown sugar, paprika, cayenne powder (if using), salt, and pepper and cook for 5 minutes more. Taste and season to your preferences. Transfer the mushroom mixture to a bowl and let it cool for 20 minutes. You can use a spoon to spread the mixture around the sides of the bowl to allow it to cool more quickly and evenly. Wipe out the skillet.

4. **While the black bean burger mixture cools, prepare the plantain buns:** Peel the plantains and transfer them to a bowl. Use a fork to mash them until they are almost completely mush. It's okay if they're a little lumpy. Season with salt and chili powder. Add the cassava flour and work it into the mixture until it is thick and pasty. If it seems too wet, add a touch more flour. Divide the mixture into four equal portions. Heat 1 tablespoon avocado oil in your wiped-out skillet over medium-high heat. Add the first quarter of the plantain mixture and use the back of your spoon to smooth it out into a cake as it fries. Allow it to fry undisturbed for 1 to 3 minutes until golden brown. Carefully flip it and cook for 1 to 3 minutes more. Transfer to a plate. Continue frying the rest of the mixture in increments until all plantains are fried. Set aside. Wipe out the skillet.

5. **Make the black bean burgers:** Heat another teaspoon or two of avocado oil in the skillet. Turn the heat to medium. Divide the black bean mixture into four equal portions. The mixture should hold together, but if it seems too wet, add a touch more flour. Form the four portions of the mixture into patties. Transfer the first burger to the hot skillet and allow it to cook undisturbed for 3 to 4 minutes. Carefully flip and cook for another 2 to 4 minutes until well-browned. Transfer to a plate. Continue cooking the patties in batches.

6. **To serve:** Place a plantain bun on a plate and spread a spoonful of chipotle mayonnaise on top. Place a black bean burger on top and garnish with the tomatillo salsa. Enjoy!

PLAN 3: WEEK 2

This recipe plan includes dinner recipes for five days, all of which serve four. To conquer the grocery store in one shopping trip, the next page outlines a detailed grocery list, with items separated by store department. You will also find storage, freezing, and thawing tips to help you plan your week. This plan relishes a slower pace to create the fullest flavors. Pay special attention to the key players throughout the week (tomatoes and leeks) and be sure to buy the freshest and healthiest of those ingredients that you can find, because you will use them for multiple recipes.

THE MENU

MONDAY
Braised Kale and White Bean Soup

TUESDAY
Poached Tomatoes and White Beans

WEDNESDAY
Tomato-Oil Risotto with Roasted
Acorn Squash

THURSDAY
Creamy Beet Pappardelle

FRIDAY
Soba in Wasabi Broth

PLAN 3: WEEK 2
CONQUERING THE GROCERY STORE

FOOD SAFETY GUIDELINES

Buying groceries for the entire week can require some forethought, so be sure to refer to the FDA's storage and freezing guidelines for your ingredients. To keep herbs and leafy greens fresh through the week, wrap them in a damp paper towel and store in a bag in your crisper. Refresh the paper towel periodically through the week to keep them extra fresh.

PLANT-BASED PROTEIN
- ☐ 1 pound extra-firm tofu

GRAINS
- ☐ 1 cup uncooked carnaroli or arborio rice

OIL
- ☐ Avocado oil
- ☐ Extra-virgin olive oil

PLANT-BASED DAIRY
- ☐ ½ cup plant-based Greek yogurt

STOCK
- ☐ 26 cups vegetable stock

FRUITS & VEGETABLES
- ☐ 2 yellow onions
- ☐ 2 heads garlic
- ☐ 3 leeks
- ☐ 1 pound mixed mushrooms
- ☐ 2 pounds (8 whole) tomatoes
- ☐ 1 pound cherry or grape tomatoes
- ☐ 1 red Fresno chili pepper
- ☐ 1 acorn squash
- ☐ 1 bunch Lacinato kale
- ☐ 3 red beets with greens
- ☐ 1 lemon
- ☐ ½ cup parsley

PANTRY & SPICES
- ☐ 16 ounces pappardelle
- ☐ 16 ounces soba
- ☐ 4 (15-ounce) cans navy beans
- ☐ Wasabi paste
- ☐ Chili oil
- ☐ Mirin
- ☐ White miso paste
- ☐ Soy sauce
- ☐ Sesame oil
- ☐ Dry thyme
- ☐ Sweet paprika
- ☐ Smoked paprika
- ☐ Sesame seeds
- ☐ Shichimi-togarashi, optional
- ☐ Salt
- ☐ Pepper
- ☐ Crushed red pepper

Braised Kale and White Bean Soup

Time to Make: 55 minutes (35 minutes inactive)

Serves: 4

WHY THIS RECIPE WORKS

The broth in this white bean soup will taste like it simmered for hours thanks to plenty of fragrant aromatics, including a sliced leek and dry thyme. The real secret ingredient is the smoked paprika. It creates a surprising smoky undertone that pairs perfectly with tender white beans and braised kale.

SUBSTITUTIONS

Leek: Yellow onion or green garlic if it is in season
Lacinato kale: Curly kale, red Russian kale, Swiss chard, or mustard greens

EQUIPMENT & LEFTOVERS

You'll need: Large pot and Microplane
Leftovers: Store in an airtight container in the fridge for 3 days

INGREDIENTS

1 tablespoon avocado oil

1 leek, thinly sliced into rounds

8 cloves garlic, peeled and minced

1 teaspoon dry thyme

1 teaspoon sweet paprika

1 teaspoon smoked paprika

2 (15-ounce) cans navy beans, drained

Salt and pepper to taste

6 cups vegetable stock

1 bunch Lacinato kale, stems removed and leaves
   roughly chopped

1 lemon, juiced and zested

Crushed red pepper, optional, for garnish

METHOD

1. **Prepare the soup:** Heat the avocado oil in a large soup pot over medium-high heat. Add the leek and cook, stirring regularly, for 7 to 8 minutes until softened. Add the garlic, dry thyme, sweet paprika, and smoked paprika and cook for 1 minute until fragrant. Add the beans and toss to combine. Season with salt and pepper. Pour in the vegetable stock and bring to a boil. Reduce heat and simmer for 25 minutes. Stir the kale into the soup and cover the pot. Simmer for 15 minutes until tender.

2. **Right before serving, add the lemon juice and zest to the pot:** Taste and season it to your preferences.

3. **To serve:** Ladle the soup into bowls and garnish with crushed red pepper, if desired. Enjoy!

Poached Tomatoes and White Beans

Time to Make: 50 minutes (20 minutes inactive)

Serves: 4

WHY THIS RECIPE WORKS

Use any variety of tomatoes that you like in this recipe but adding a few larger tomatoes into the mix makes it easier to scoop them out for the tomato oil.

SUBSTITUTIONS

Tomatoes: If tomatoes are not in season, use canned tomatoes and omit the tomato oil
Leek: Yellow onion or green garlic if it is in season

EQUIPMENT & LEFTOVERS

You'll need: Wide pot, fine-mesh sieve, and whisk
Leftovers: Store Poached Tomatoes and White Beans in an airtight container in the fridge for 3 days, and store leftover tomato oil in a separate, airtight container in the fridge for 7 days and whisk right before using

INGREDIENTS

2 tablespoons + ½ cup extra-virgin olive oil, divided

1 tablespoon chili oil, optional

2 pounds (8 whole) tomatoes

1 pound cherry or grape tomatoes

Salt, pepper, and crushed red pepper to taste

4–5 cups vegetable stock plus more as needed to cover the tomatoes

2 (15-ounce) cans navy beans, drained

1 leek, thinly sliced

METHOD

1. **Start the tomatoes:** Add 2 tablespoons extra-virgin olive oil and chili oil (if using) to a wide pot. Add tomatoes and turn the heat to medium. Season with salt and pepper.

2. **Simmer the tomatoes:** Once the oil sizzles slightly, pour in the vegetable stock and bring to a low boil. Reduce heat and simmer, uncovered, for 30 minutes.

3. **Make the tomato oil:** Remove 4 of the larger tomatoes and transfer to a bowl. Carefully remove the skins and discard them. Mash the tomatoes in the bowl. Place a fine-mesh sieve over an empty bowl and pour the mashed tomatoes into the sieve. Use a fork to mash out any tomato liquid. Discard any leftover tomato pulp. To the tomato liquid, whisk in remaining extra-virgin olive oil until completely emulsified. Season with salt and set aside. (Note: You may need to whisk again right before serving.)

4. **Simmer the beans:** Add the beans and the leek to the simmering tomatoes and cook for 20 to 25 minutes until the beans are soft. Taste and season with salt, pepper, and crushed red pepper, if desired.

5. **To serve:** Divide the beans and broth between shallow bowls. Arrange a few cherry or grape tomatoes on each dish and serve each person a larger tomato in the broth as well. Drizzle with tomato oil. Enjoy!

Tomato-Oil Risotto with Roasted Acorn Squash

Time to Make: 50 minutes

Serves: 4

WHY THIS RECIPE WORKS
Use the rest of your tomato oil from yesterday's recipe in this beautiful rose-colored risotto. If you do not have tomato oil, simply use 3 tablespoons plant-based butter in its place.

SUBSTITUTIONS
Acorn squash: Butternut squash, sweet potatoes, or delicata squash
Leek: Yellow onion or green garlic if it is in season

EQUIPMENT & LEFTOVERS
You'll need: Baking sheet and medium pot
Leftovers: Store in an airtight container in the fridge for 3 days

INGREDIENTS
1 acorn squash, halved, seeded, and sliced into half-moons

2 tablespoons avocado oil, divided

Salt and pepper to taste

1 leek, thinly sliced

4 cloves garlic, peeled and minced

⅓ cup tomato oil (see previous recipe for recipe instructions)

1 cup uncooked carnaroli or arborio rice

3–6 cups warm vegetable stock, divided

METHOD
1. **Preheat oven to 400°F.**

2. **Prepare the squash:** Arrange the squash on a baking sheet and drizzle with 1 tablespoon avocado oil. Season with salt and pepper. Transfer to the oven and roast for 25 to 30 minutes, flipping once halfway through. Turn off the heat and keep the squash in the warm oven as you finish the risotto.

3. **Cook the risotto:** Heat remaining avocado oil in a medium pot over medium-high heat. Add the leek and cook, stirring often, for 6 to 7 minutes until softened. Add the garlic and cook for 45 seconds until fragrant. Add the tomato oil and stir to incorporate. Once the tomato oil begins to bubble, add the carnaroli rice and toss to coat. Cook for 1 to 2 minutes. Ladle in 1 cup warm vegetable stock. Cook for 2 to 3 minutes until most of the liquid is absorbed. Continue adding stock, alternating stirring and disturbing the rice until the rice is al dente and soft. Be patient! It will take about 30 to 35 minutes total. You may use all the stock or only 3 to 4 cups. Continue stirring until the rice is softened and the sauce is velvety and luxurious. Taste and season with salt and pepper. Turn off the heat and allow the risotto to rest for 5 minutes.

4. **To serve:** Divide the risotto between plates and arrange the roasted squash on top. Garnish with a drizzle of tomato oil. Enjoy!

Creamy Beet Pappardelle

Time to Make: 45 minutes

Serves: 4

WHY THIS RECIPE WORKS

The genius of this recipe is using the entire beet, including the greens. The beets are peeled, cubed, and simmered with aromatics, then blended into a smooth sauce. The greens are finely minced and tossed with fresh herbs, lemon juice, and extra-virgin olive oil. Serve the beet-soaked pappardelle with the beet green salad on top as a bright and herby finish.

SUBSTITUTIONS

Red Fresno chili pepper: Your favorite hot pepper, such as habanero, jalapeño, or serrano pepper, or crushed red pepper to taste
Red beets: Golden beets
Plant-based Greek yogurt: Plant-based cream cheese or plant-based sour cream
Pappardelle: Tagliatelle or linguine

EQUIPMENT & LEFTOVERS

You'll need: Wide pot, large pot, and colander
Leftovers: Store in an airtight container in the fridge for 3 days

INGREDIENTS

2 tablespoons avocado oil
1 yellow onion, peeled and diced
5 cloves garlic, peeled and minced
1 red Fresno chili pepper, minced
3 red beets, peeled and cubed, beet greens reserved
Salt and pepper to taste
3 cups vegetable stock or water
2 tablespoons extra-virgin olive oil
½ cup fresh parsley, minced
16 ounces pappardelle
½ cup plant-based Greek yogurt

METHOD

1. **Start the beet sauce:** Heat the avocado oil in a wide pot over medium heat. Add the onion and cook for 5 minutes until it softens. Add garlic and red Fresno chili pepper and cook for 1 minute until fragrant. Add the beets and cook for 2 minutes. Season with salt and pepper. Pour in the vegetable stock or water and bring to a boil. Reduce heat to low. Cover and simmer for 30 minutes until the beets are very soft.

2. **Meanwhile, prepare the beet green salad:** Wash the beet greens thoroughly and gently squeeze out the water. Very thinly slice and transfer to a bowl. Drizzle with extra-virgin olive oil and massage the oil into the greens. Add the parsley and season with salt and pepper.

3. **Cook the pasta:** Bring a large pot of salted water to a boil and cook the pasta according to package instructions. Reserve ½ cup cooking water. Drain and set aside.

4. **Finish the beet sauce:** Once the beets are very tender, add a touch more stock or water if needed and use an immersion blender or blender to pulse until smooth. Taste and season to your preferences. Add the plant-based Greek yogurt to the beet sauce and stir to incorporate. Add the reserved pasta water and the cooked pasta and toss to coat until the pasta is bright pink.

5. **To serve:** Divide the pasta between bowls and pile the beet green salad on top. Enjoy!

Soba in Wasabi Broth

Time to Make: 40 minutes

Serves: 4

WHY THIS RECIPE WORKS

Loaded with nose-tingling spicy wasabi, the heat in this broth is softened with lots of tofu and plenty of sautéed mixed mushrooms. Use as much or as little wasabi paste as you like.

SUBSTITUTIONS

Tofu: Seitan
White miso paste: Red miso paste
Soba: Udon or ramen noodles

EQUIPMENT & LEFTOVERS

You'll need: Heavy object to press the tofu, paper towels, whisk, large pot, colander, medium pot, and skillet
Leftovers: Store the broth, tofu, and mushrooms together in an airtight container in the fridge for 3 days, and drizzle leftover noodles with a touch of sesame oil and store them separately from the broth in an airtight container in the fridge for 3–5 days

INGREDIENTS

1 pound extra-firm tofu

1–2 tablespoons wasabi paste

2 tablespoons mirin

1 tablespoon white miso paste

1 tablespoon soy sauce

1 teaspoon sesame oil

2 tablespoons + 2 teaspoons avocado oil, divided

1 yellow onion, peeled and thinly sliced

6 cups vegetable stock

16 ounces soba

1 pound mixed mushrooms

Salt and pepper to taste

1 teaspoon sesame seeds

Shichimi-togarashi, for serving, optional

METHOD

1. **Press the tofu:** Wrap the tofu in paper towels on a plate. Place a heavy object (like a book) on top of the tofu for 20 minutes, then cut into bite-sized cubes.

2. **Prepare the wasabi broth base:** Whisk together the wasabi, mirin, miso, soy sauce, and sesame oil.

3. **Prepare the wasabi broth:** Heat 1 tablespoon avocado oil in a large pot over medium heat. Add the onion and cook, stirring often, for 8 minutes until it begins to soften. Pour in the vegetable stock and bring to a boil. Reduce heat to a simmer and stir in the wasabi soup base. Simmer for 20 to 30 minutes.

4. **Cook the soba noodles:** Bring a medium pot of salted water to a boil and cook soba noodles according to package instructions. Drain and rinse.

5. **Fry the mushrooms:** Heat 1 tablespoon avocado oil in a skillet. Add mixed mushrooms, in batches if needed, and cook for 8 to 10 minutes until beginning to brown and crisp up around the edges. Season with salt and pepper and transfer to a bowl. Wipe out the skillet.

6. **Fry the tofu:** In the same skillet add the remaining avocado oil and tofu in an even layer. Fry for 3 to 5 minutes per side until golden brown all over. Sprinkle sesame seeds on a plate and transfer the fried tofu to the plate. Season with salt and pepper and toss until the tofu is lightly coated with sesame seeds.

7. **To serve:** Divide cooked noodles between bowls and ladle the hot wasabi broth on top. Pile the tofu and mushrooms on each bowl and sprinkle with shichimi-togarashi, if desired.

PLAN 3: WEEK 3

This recipe plan includes dinner recipes for five days, all of which serve four. To conquer the grocery store in one shopping trip, the next page outlines a detailed grocery list, with items separated by store department. You will also find storage, freezing, and thawing tips to help you plan your week. This plan is the meanest, greenest plan out of the pack! Pay special attention to the key players throughout the week (lots of fresh herbs like cilantro, Thai basil, mint, and tarragon) and be sure to buy the freshest and healthiest of those ingredients that you can find, because you will use them for multiple recipes.

THE MENU

MONDAY
Rice Noodles with Cilantro and Lime

TUESDAY
Vegan Roasted Poblano-Corn Chowder

WEDNESDAY
White Wine Potatoes and Arugula

THURSDAY
Broccoli and "Cheese" Grits

FRIDAY
Mushroom-Macadamia Burrito Bowl

PLAN 3: WEEK 3
CONQUERING THE GROCERY STORE

FOOD SAFETY GUIDELINES

Buying groceries for the entire week can require some forethought, so be sure to refer to the FDA's storage and freezing guidelines for your ingredients. To keep herbs and leafy greens fresh through the week, wrap them in a damp paper towel and store in a bag in your crisper. Refresh the paper towel periodically through the week to keep them extra fresh.

GRAINS
- ☐ 1 cup uncooked white rice
- ☐ 1 cup yellow corn grits

OIL
- ☐ Avocado oil
- ☐ Extra-virgin olive oil

PLANT-BASED DAIRY
- ☐ 6 tablespoons plant-based butter
- ☐ ¼ cup oat milk
- ☐ ½ cup plant-based ricotta cheese
- ☐ ½ cup vegan parmesan cheese
- ☐ ½ cup vegan cheddar cheese

STOCK
- ☐ 12 cups vegetable stock
- ☐ 1 cup white wine or vegetable stock

FRUITS & VEGETABLES
- ☐ 4 yellow onions
- ☐ 1 red onion
- ☐ 2 heads garlic
- ☐ 1 pound Yukon Gold potatoes
- ☐ 6 king trumpet mushrooms
- ☐ 4 jalapeño peppers
- ☐ 3 poblano peppers
- ☐ 1 red Fresno chili pepper
- ☐ 6 ears husked corn or 16 ounces frozen corn
- ☐ 12 ounces sugar snap peas
- ☐ 1 pound broccoli florets
- ☐ 1 head curly kale
- ☐ 4 ounces watercress
- ☐ 5 ounces arugula
- ☐ 2 large tomatoes
- ☐ 1 pint cherry tomatoes
- ☐ 1 lemon
- ☐ 4 limes
- ☐ 1½ cups cilantro
- ☐ 1 ounce Thai basil
- ☐ ½ ounce mint leaves
- ☐ ¼ ounce fresh tarragon
- ☐ ¼ cup parsley
- ☐ 2 avocados

PANTRY & SPICES
- ☐ 1 (15-ounce) can coconut milk
- ☐ 1 (15-ounce) can chickpeas
- ☐ 1 (15-ounce) can black beans
- ☐ 8 ounces medium rice noodles
- ☐ 4 ounces blanched macadamia nuts
- ☐ Sesame oil
- ☐ Chili powder
- ☐ Garlic powder
- ☐ Paprika
- ☐ Mexican oregano
- ☐ Smoked paprika
- ☐ White pepper
- ☐ Cayenne powder
- ☐ Cumin powder
- ☐ Salt
- ☐ Pepper
- ☐ Crushed red pepper
- ☐ Soy sauce

Rice Noodles with Cilantro and Lime

Time to Make: 20 minutes

Serves: 4

WHY THIS RECIPE WORKS

This recipe comes together in a cool twenty minutes. Simply prepare an herby, bright, spicy vinaigrette and toss it with cooked rice noodles. The easiest, breeziest part? Tossing the sugar snap peas in with the noodles right as they finish cooking to quickly blanch them. Throw it all together in a bowl with your vinaigrette, and you'll be ready to eat in no time.

SUBSTITUTIONS

Rice noodles: Soba or glass noodles (cook time will vary)
Sugar snap peas: Asparagus, snow peas, or chopped broccoli
Watercress: Your favorite microgreen or baby spinach, arugula, or baby kale

EQUIPMENT & LEFTOVERS

You'll need: Large pot, colander, and food processor
Leftovers: Store together in an airtight container in the fridge for 3 days

INGREDIENTS

8 ounces medium rice noodles

12 ounces sugar snap peas, de-stringed

3 teaspoons sesame oil, divided

Salt and pepper to taste

2 limes

1 cup cilantro, loosely packed

½ ounce Thai basil leaves

1 jalapeño, stem removed, plus extra for garnish

1 tablespoon soy sauce

4 tablespoons extra-virgin olive oil

4 ounces watercress, plus extra for garnish

METHOD

1. **Prepare the rice noodles:** Bring a large pot of water to a boil. Add the rice noodles and cook for 6 minutes until almost tender but still chewy. Add the sugar snap peas and cook for 1 to 2 minutes until bright green. Drain the noodles and sugar snap peas into a colander and immediately rinse with cold water. Transfer to a large bowl and drizzle with 2 teaspoons sesame oil and a sprinkle of salt and toss to coat.

2. **Prepare the vinaigrette:** Juice the limes into a food processor. Add the cilantro, Thai basil, and jalapeño and pulse until minced. Add the soy sauce, remaining sesame oil, and extra-virgin olive oil and continue pulsing until completely emulsified. Taste and season with salt and pepper.

3. **Finish the rice noodles:** Pour the vinaigrette over the rice noodles and sugar snap peas and toss to coat. Add the watercress to the bowl and toss until everything is combined.

4. **To serve:** Divide the noodles between bowls and garnish with a few watercress leaves and jalapeño slices on each bowl, if desired. Enjoy!

Vegan Roasted Poblano-Corn Chowder

Time to Make: 60 minutes

Serves: 4

WHY THIS RECIPE WORKS

This roasted poblano-corn chowder is loaded with corn, kale, and roasted peppers for a hearty soup you can eat any time of year.

SUBSTITUTIONS

Poblano peppers: Tomatillos

EQUIPMENT & LEFTOVERS

You'll need: Baking sheet, food processor, large pot, and immersion blender (optional)
Leftovers: Store in an airtight container in the fridge for 3 days

INGREDIENTS

3 poblano peppers, seeds removed

1 jalapeño, halved

6 cloves garlic, peeled

3 teaspoons avocado oil, divided

Salt, pepper, and cayenne powder to taste

6 ears corn, husked, or 16 ounces frozen corn, plus extra for garnish

1 yellow onion, peeled and diced

5 cups vegetable stock

1 head curly kale, stems discarded, leaves torn into bite-sized pieces

1 (15-ounce) can coconut milk

1 avocado peeled, sliced, and pit removed

Crushed red pepper to taste

METHOD

1. **Preheat oven to 425°F.**

2. **Prepare the peppers:** Arrange the poblano peppers, jalapeño, and garlic on a baking sheet. Drizzle with 2 teaspoons avocado oil and a sprinkle of salt. Transfer to the oven for 20 minutes until the skins of the peppers blister and char. Remove from the oven and let cool for 5 to 10 minutes. Once the poblano peppers are cool enough to handle, carefully remove the skins and stems. Remove the stem from the jalapeño pepper. Transfer the poblano peppers, jalapeño, and garlic to a food processor and pulse until finely chopped. Alternatively, you can roughly chop the peppers and garlic with a knife.

3. **Start the chowder:** Heat the remaining avocado oil in a large pot. Add the onion and cook for 4 to 5 minutes until just beginning to soften. Add the finely chopped roasted peppers and garlic and cook for 3 to 5 minutes more until very fragrant. Add the vegetable stock and bring to a boil. Reduce heat.

4. **Simmer the chowder:** Add half the corn, the coconut milk, and the kale leaves. Simmer for 10 to 15 minutes until softened. Taste and season with salt, pepper, and cayenne powder.

(Continued on page 172)

5. **Blend the chowder:** Using an immersion blender, blend the soup until smooth and creamy. Note: If you do not have an immersion blender, you can skip this step. Taste and season again to your tastes.

6. **Finish the chowder:** Add the remaining half of the corn and simmer for 10 minutes more. Taste and season. Turn off heat.

7. **To serve:** Ladle the chowder into bowls and arrange reserved fresh sweet corn and sliced avocado on top. Sprinkle with crushed red pepper, if desired. Enjoy!

White Wine Potatoes and Arugula

Time to Make: 45 minutes (20 minutes inactive)

Serves: 4

WHY THIS RECIPE WORKS

A simple white wine broth is paired with potatoes and herby, bright chickpeas for an amazingly simple dinner recipe that doesn't hold back on flavor.

SUBSTITUTIONS

Chickpeas: Your favorite white bean, such as navy, great northern, or cannellini beans
Yukon Gold potatoes: Russet potatoes or sweet potatoes
Arugula: Spinach or baby kale
Red Fresno chili pepper: Your favorite hot pepper, such as habanero, jalapeño, or serrano pepper, or crushed red pepper to taste

EQUIPMENT & LEFTOVERS

You'll need: Wide pot and Microplane
Leftovers: Store together in an airtight container in the fridge for 3 days

INGREDIENTS

2 teaspoons avocado oil

1 yellow onion, peeled and thinly sliced

2 tablespoons plant-based butter

1 pound Yukon Gold potatoes, medium-diced

Salt and pepper to taste

½ cup white wine or vegetable stock

4 cups vegetable stock

1 (15-ounce) can chickpeas, drained

2 tablespoons extra-virgin olive oil

1 lemon, juiced and zested

½ ounce mint leaves, roughly chopped, plus a few leaves reserved for garnish

½ ounce Thai basil leaves, roughly chopped, plus a few leaves reserved for garnish

¼ ounce fresh tarragon, roughly chopped

1 red Fresno chili pepper, thinly sliced into rounds

5 ounces arugula

(Continued on page 175)

METHOD

1. **Start the broth:** Heat the avocado oil in a wide pot over medium heat. Add the onions and cook, stirring often, for 8 minutes until softened and beginning to brown. Melt the plant-based butter into the onions and add the potatoes. Cook for 4 minutes until just beginning to turn golden brown in places. Season liberally with salt and pepper.

2. **Simmer the potatoes:** Add the ½ cup white wine or vegetable stock to the pot and bring to a boil. Add the 4 cups vegetable stock. Reduce heat to medium-low and simmer for 20 minutes or until potatoes are fork tender. Add more stock as necessary and taste and season with salt and pepper.

3. **Meanwhile, prepare the chickpeas:** Combine the chickpeas, extra-virgin olive oil, lemon juice, zest, and salt and pepper in a bowl and toss to coat. Add mint, Thai basil, tarragon, and the red Fresno chili pepper and toss to coat. Taste and season with salt and pepper. Set aside.

4. **Right before serving, stir the arugula into the potatoes:** Taste and season lightly with salt and pepper. Turn off the heat once the arugula is wilted.

5. **To serve:** Ladle the potatoes and broth into bowls. Pile the herby chickpeas on top. Garnish with reserved mint and Thai basil leaves. Enjoy!

Broccoli and "Cheese" Grits

Time to Make: 40 minutes

Serves: 4

WHY THIS RECIPE WORKS

Broccoli and cheese . . . name a more iconic duo. Instead of the classic soup, this recipe combines sautéed broccoli and tomatoes over the creamiest vegan grits. Use your favorite vegan cheese, but we recommend vegan ricotta and vegan cheddar for the best creamy, cheesy grits.

SUBSTITUTIONS

Broccoli: Asparagus or eggplant (cook time will vary)
Cherry tomatoes: 1 (15-ounce) can strained whole peeled tomatoes

EQUIPMENT & LEFTOVERS

You'll need: Ovenproof skillet, medium pot, and whisk
Leftovers: Store in an airtight container in the fridge for 3 days

INGREDIENTS

1 tablespoon avocado oil

1 yellow onion, peeled and thinly sliced

1 pound broccoli, cut into florets

Salt, pepper, and crushed red pepper to taste

1 pint cherry tomatoes

1 teaspoon extra-virgin olive oil

6 cloves garlic, minced

4 tablespoons plant-based butter

½ cup dry white wine or vegetable stock

1 cup vegetable stock

3 cups water

1 cup yellow corn grits

¼ cup oat milk

½ cup plant-based ricotta cheese

½ cup vegan parmesan cheese

½ cup vegan cheddar cheese

¼ cup fresh parsley, minced, for garnish

(Continued on page 178)

METHOD

1. **Preheat oven to 425°F.**

2. **Prepare the broccoli:** Heat the avocado oil in an ovenproof skillet over medium heat. Add the yellow onion and cook for 6 to 8 minutes until it begins to soften. Add the broccoli and cook for 2 minutes. Season with salt and pepper. Add the tomatoes and drizzle with the extra-virgin olive oil. Season tomatoes with salt and pepper. Transfer the skillet to the oven for 20 to 25 minutes or until the broccoli and tomatoes begin to char. Remove the broccoli from the oven and transfer to the stove. Carefully mash the tomatoes into the broccoli.

3. **Finish the broccoli:** Turn the heat on the broccoli to medium. Add garlic and cook for 1 minute. Melt the plant-based butter into the skillet. Add a sprinkle of crushed red pepper. Once frothy, add the ½ cup white wine or vegetable stock and 1 cup vegetable stock. Bring to a boil, then reduce heat to medium and cook until thickened and reduced, about 6 to 7 minutes. Taste and season to your preferences. Turn off the heat.

4. **While the broccoli roasts, cook the grits:** Bring 3 cups of salted water to a boil and stir in the corn grits. Whisk regularly for 25 to 30 minutes until tender.

5. **Finish the grits:** Stir in the oat milk, plant-based ricotta cheese, vegan parmesan, and vegan cheddar and season to taste with salt and pepper.

6. **To serve:** Divide the grits between bowls and pile the broccoli on top. Garnish with parsley.

Mushroom-Macadamia Burrito Bowl

Time to Make: 30 minutes

Serves: 4

WHY THIS RECIPE WORKS

This burrito bowl is unbelievably easy to prepare. Lightly crushed macadamia nuts add a rich protein to the mushrooms and beans.

SUBSTITUTIONS

King trumpet mushroom: Any mushroom variety, such as cremini, baby bella, oyster, or shitake
Macadamia nuts: Cashews, walnuts, or hazelnuts

EQUIPMENT & LEFTOVERS

You'll need: Small pot and wide pot
Leftovers: Store in an airtight container in the fridge for 3 days

INGREDIENTS

1 cup uncooked white rice

2 cups water

Salt and pepper to taste

1 tablespoon avocado oil

1 yellow onion, peeled and diced

6 king trumpet mushrooms, diced

4 ounces blanched macadamia nuts, lightly crushed

1 tablespoon cumin powder

1 tablespoon chili powder

2 teaspoons garlic powder

2 teaspoons paprika

1 teaspoon Mexican oregano

1 teaspoon smoked paprika

½ teaspoon cayenne powder

¼ teaspoon white pepper, optional

1 (15-ounce) can black beans, drained

2 cups vegetable stock

1 red onion, peeled and finely diced

2 large tomatoes, chopped

½ cup loosely packed cilantro, roughly chopped

1 jalapeño, minced

4 cloves garlic, peeled and minced

2 limes, divided

Sliced avocado

(Continued on page 181)

METHOD

1. **Cook the rice:** Combine rice, water, and a pinch of salt in a small pot and bring to a boil. Stir once. Cover, reduce heat, and simmer for 15 minutes. Turn off the heat and allow the rice to rest for 10 minutes, then remove the lid and fluff with a fork.

2. **Start the mushrooms:** Heat the avocado oil in a wide pot over medium heat. Add the onion and sauté for 5 minutes. Add the mushrooms and cook for 8 minutes, stirring occasionally. Season with salt and pepper. Add the macadamia nuts and toss to combine. Add the cumin powder, chili powder, garlic powder, paprika, Mexican oregano, smoked paprika, cayenne powder, and white pepper (if using) to the mushrooms. Cook for 1 minute.

3. **Simmer the mushrooms:** Add the black beans and vegetable stock to the pot and bring to a boil. Reduce heat and simmer for 20 to 25 minutes. Add more water as necessary to loosen up the mushrooms if they stick to the pot. Taste and season to your preferences.

4. **Prepare the pico de gallo:** Combine the red onion, tomatoes, jalapeño, garlic, and cilantro in a bowl. Add the juice from 1 lime and season with salt. Toss to combine.

5. **To serve:** Divide the cooked rice between bowls. Pile the cooked mushrooms and pico de gallo on top. Garnish with sliced avocado and serve with a lime wedge. Enjoy!

PLAN 3: WEEK 4

This recipe plan includes dinner recipes for five days, all of which serve four. To conquer the grocery store in one shopping trip, the next page outlines a detailed grocery list, with items separated by store department. You will also find storage, freezing, and thawing tips to help you plan your week. This plan has a little bit of everything in it, from light and bright to stewed and comforting and everything in between. Pay special attention to the key players throughout the week (bok choy and shitake mushrooms) and be sure to buy the freshest and healthiest of those ingredients that you can find, because you will use them for multiple recipes.

THE MENU

MONDAY
Bok Choy Wraps with Tofu

TUESDAY
Stewed Lentils with Sweet Potato Hummus

WEDNESDAY
Noodle Salad with Spicy Pickled Tomatoes

THURSDAY
Pumpkin Red Lentil Bolognese

FRIDAY
Spicy Beans with Mashed Celeriac

PLAN 3: WEEK 4
CONQUERING THE GROCERY STORE

FOOD SAFETY GUIDELINES

Buying groceries for the entire week can require some forethought, so be sure to refer to the FDA's storage and freezing guidelines for your ingredients. To keep herbs and leafy greens fresh through the week, wrap them in a damp paper towel and store in a bag in your crisper. Refresh the paper towel periodically through the week to keep them extra fresh.

PLANT-BASED PROTEIN

☐ 1 pound extra-firm tofu

GRAINS

☐ 1 cup uncooked white rice

OIL

☐ Avocado oil

☐ Extra-virgin olive oil

PLANT-BASED DAIRY

☐ ½ cup plant-based Greek yogurt

☐ ¾ cup plant-based sour cream

☐ 2 tablespoons plant-based butter

☐ Oat milk, as needed

STOCK

☐ 8½ cups vegetable stock

FRUITS & VEGETABLES

☐ 4 yellow onions

☐ 2 shallots

☐ 1 leek

☐ 16 ounces shitake mushrooms

☐ 12 ounces cremini mushrooms

☐ 2 pounds celeriac (celery root)

☐ 1 pound (4 whole) Yukon Gold potatoes

☐ 1½ pounds (2 whole) sweet potatoes

☐ 7 heads baby bok choy (look for bok choy that is about 6 to 7 inches in length)

☐ 1 red bell pepper

☐ 1 seedless cucumber

☐ 1 pint cherry tomatoes

☐ 1 orange

☐ 7 scallions

☐ ½ ounce sage

☐ ½ cup cilantro

☐ ½ cup parsley

(Continued on next page)

PANTRY & SPICES

- ☐ 1 (15-ounce) can chickpeas
- ☐ 1 (15-ounce) can pumpkin puree
- ☐ 2 (15-ounce) cans great northern beans
- ☐ 1 cup French green lentils
- ☐ ½ cup red lentils
- ☐ 12 ounces cellophane noodles
- ☐ 16 ounces orecchiette
- ☐ 2 tablespoons tomato paste
- ☐ ½ cup raw pumpkin seeds
- ☐ Tahini
- ☐ Rice vinegar
- ☐ Sugar
- ☐ Brown sugar or maple syrup
- ☐ Sesame oil
- ☐ Soy sauce
- ☐ 1 (15-ounce) can crushed tomatoes
- ☐ Chili oil
- ☐ Dry thyme
- ☐ Garlic powder
- ☐ Ground ginger
- ☐ Ground cinnamon
- ☐ Smoked paprika
- ☐ Chili powder
- ☐ Sweet paprika
- ☐ Cayenne powder
- ☐ Black sesame seeds
- ☐ Chinese five spice powder
- ☐ Dried parsley
- ☐ Ground nutmeg
- ☐ Flaky sea salt
- ☐ Salt
- ☐ Pepper
- ☐ White pepper
- ☐ Crushed red pepper

Bok Choy Wraps with Tofu

Time to Make: 40 minutes

Serves: 4

WHY THIS RECIPE WORKS

This recipe is so easy to make. If you're not in the mood for wraps, simply chop up all of the bok choy and add it to the mushroom filling and serve over rice.

SUBSTITUTIONS

Shitake mushrooms: Any mushroom variety, such as cremini, baby bella, oyster, or maitake
Baby bok choy: 1 head bok choy or 1 head tatsoi but omit the wraps and chop the greens into the filling

EQUIPMENT & LEFTOVERS

You'll need: Small pot and wide pot
Leftovers: Store in an airtight container in the fridge for 3 days

INGREDIENTS

1 pound extra-firm tofu

1 cup uncooked white rice

2 cups water

Salt and pepper to taste

4 heads baby bok choy (look for bok choy that is about 6 to 7 inches in length), divided

1 tablespoon avocado oil

1 yellow onion, peeled and diced

10 ounces shitake mushrooms, caps diced

1 teaspoon Chinese five spice powder

1 tablespoon sesame oil

2 tablespoons soy sauce

½ cup vegetable stock

1 teaspoon black sesame seeds

Chili oil, optional, for serving

METHOD

1. **Press the tofu:** Wrap the tofu in paper towels on a plate. Place a heavy object (like a book) on top of the tofu for 20 minutes. Dice the tofu into small pieces and set aside.

2. **Cook the rice:** Combine rice, water, and a pinch of salt in a small pot and bring to a boil. Stir once. Cover, reduce heat, and simmer for 15 minutes. Turn off the heat and allow the rice to rest for 10 minutes, then remove the lid and fluff with a fork.

3. **Prepare the bok choy:** Remove 8 of the biggest and best leaves from the bok choy and set aside for the wraps. Finely chop the remaining bok choy and set aside.

4. **Start the mushroom filling:** Heat the avocado oil in a wide pot over medium heat. Add the onion and cook for 8 to 10 minutes until it softens and begins to brown. Add the shitake mushrooms and cook for an additional 8 to 10 minutes. Once the mushrooms begin to turn golden brown around the edges, add the tofu and break it up as you cook for 5 to 6 minutes. It should crumble a bit as it cooks.

(Continued on page 187)

5. **Finish the mushroom filling:** Add the Chinese five spice powder to the mushrooms and cook for 1 minute until fragrant. Add the sesame oil, soy sauce, and chopped bok choy. Add the vegetable stock and bring to a boil. Reduce heat and simmer for 15 minutes. Taste and season to your preferences. Turn off the heat and add the black sesame seeds right before serving.

6. **To serve:** Divide the cooked rice between plates. Fill each of the bok choy leaves with mushroom filling and arrange two wraps on top of each plate of rice. Garnish with chili oil and more sesame seeds. Serve with extra filling on the side. Enjoy!

Stewed Lentils with Sweet Potato Hummus

Time to Make: 60 minutes (20 minutes inactive)

Serves: 4

WHY THIS RECIPE WORKS

This recipe is a tour de force of flavors and textures. The sweet potato hummus is smooth, creamy, and lightly sweet while the stewed lentils are warm, rich, and aromatic. Paired with a dollop of plant-based Greek yogurt, this meal is decadent without being overly rich.

SUBSTITUTIONS

Sweet potatoes: Butternut squash or roasted red bell peppers
Orange: Lemon
Cremini mushrooms: Any mushroom variety, such as shitake, baby bella, oyster, or maitake
Leek: An yellow onion or green garlic if it is in season
French green lentils: Black lentils

EQUIPMENT & LEFTOVERS

You'll need: Baking sheet, Microplane, large pot, and food processor
Leftovers: Store in an airtight container in the fridge for 3 days

INGREDIENTS

1½ pounds (2 whole) sweet potatoes, peeled and diced into large cubes

1 tablespoon + 2 teaspoons avocado oil, divided

Salt and pepper to taste

1 yellow onion, minced

1 leek, thinly sliced

12 ounces cremini mushrooms, thinly sliced

½ ounce sage leaves, minced, plus a few leaves left whole

½ teaspoon ground nutmeg

½ teaspoon crushed red pepper

½ teaspoon ground white pepper

1 cup French green lentils

4 cups vegetable stock

1 (15-ounce) can chickpeas, drained

3 tablespoons tahini

1 orange, juiced and zested

2 teaspoons extra-virgin olive oil, plus more for garnish

½ cup plant-based Greek yogurt

Dried parsley

(Continued on page 190)

METHOD

1. **Preheat oven to 400°F.**

2. **Start the hummus:** Arrange sweet potatoes on a baking sheet and drizzle with 1 tablespoon of avocado oil. Season with salt and pepper. Roast for 40 minutes until very soft.

3. **Make the stew:** Heat remaining avocado oil in a large pot over medium heat. Add the onion and leek and cook for 10 to 12 minutes until they begin to soften and turn golden brown. Add the mushrooms to the pot and cook for 10 minutes more. Add the sage leaves, salt, pepper, nutmeg, white pepper, and crushed red pepper. Cook for 45 seconds. Add the French green lentils and cook for 1 minute. Pour in vegetable stock and bring to a boil. Reduce heat and simmer for 40 minutes, uncovered, until thickened and reduced and lentils are tender. Taste and season to preferences.

4. **Finish the hummus:** In a food processor, combine chickpeas, tahini, orange juice and zest, and 2 teaspoons extra-virgin olive oil. Pulse until blended. Add the roasted sweet potato to the food processor and pulse until smooth. Add a bit of water to thin it out to desired consistency. You should not need more than ¼ cup of water. Taste and season with salt and pepper. Set aside.

5. **Right before serving, stir in the whole sage leaves into the lentils:** Cook for 1 minute. Turn off heat.

6. **To serve:** Spoon hummus into shallow bowls and use the back of your spoon to smooth it out. Pile the stewed lentils on top. Garnish with plant-based yogurt, extra-virgin olive oil, dried parsley, and black pepper. Enjoy!

Noodle Salad with Spicy Pickled Tomatoes

Time to Make: 35 minutes

Serves: 4

WHY THIS RECIPE WORKS

The entire recipe is absolutely delicious, but the best part is that you can mash the tomatoes and coat your noodles with a delicious tomatoey sauce!

SUBSTITUTIONS

Cellophane noodles: Rice vermicelli (cook time may vary)
Shitake mushrooms: Any mushroom variety, such as cremini, baby bella, oyster, or maitake
Red bell pepper: Green bell pepper

EQUIPMENT & LEFTOVERS

You'll need: Small pot, skillet or wok, large pot, and large, microwave-safe bowl
Leftovers: Store in an airtight container in the fridge for 3 days

INGREDIENTS

¼ cup water

¼ cup + 2 tablespoons sugar, divided

½ cup rice vinegar, divided

1 tablespoon chili oil, optional

1 pint cherry tomatoes

Salt and pepper to taste

2 tablespoons avocado oil

1 yellow onion, peeled and thinly sliced into half moons

6 ounces shitake mushrooms, thinly sliced

3 heads baby bok choy, stalks thinly sliced, leafy greens shredded, stalks and greens divided

1 red bell pepper, finely diced

12 ounces cellophane noodles

3 tablespoons soy sauce

1 tablespoon sesame oil

½ cup cilantro leaves, roughly chopped

5 scallions, minced

1 seedless cucumber, thinly sliced, for garnish

(Continued on page 193)

METHOD

1. **Make the pickled tomatoes:** Combine the water and ¼ cup sugar in a small pot and turn the heat to medium. Once the sugar dissolves, add ¼ cup rice vinegar and the chili oil (if using) and add the tomatoes. Add a bit more water until the tomatoes are covered. Turn the heat to medium. Once the oil bubbles, reduce heat to low and simmer for 20 minutes. Season with a sprinkle of salt.

2. **Cook the vegetables:** Heat the avocado oil in a skillet over medium-high heat. Add the onion, shitake mushrooms, bok choy stalks, and red bell pepper in batches. Cook each batch, stirring often for 8 to 10 minutes until softened. Season with salt and pepper. Return all the vegetables back to the skillet. Stir in the bok choy leaves and cook for 2 minutes. Turn off the heat.

3. **Prepare the noodles:** Bring a large pot of water to a boil. Add the cellophane noodles and cook for 3 to 5 minutes until just soft. Drain and rinse.

4. **Prepare the noodle salad dressing:** In a large, microwave-safe bowl, combine remaining rice vinegar, the soy sauce, sesame oil, and remaining sugar. Microwave the bowl in 30-second increments until the sugar is completely dissolved. Add the cilantro and scallions and toss. Season with salt if needed.

5. **Finish the noodle salad:** Add the cooked noodles to the bowl of dressing and toss until they are coated with the dressing. Add the sautéed veggies and toss to coat. Taste and season to your preferences.

6. **To serve:** Divide the salad between plates and spoon a few pickled tomatoes on top. Garnish with cucumbers and drizzle with a spoonful of the tomato pickling liquid. Enjoy!

Pumpkin Red Lentil Bolognese

Time to Make: 55 minutes (35 minutes inactive)

Serves: 4

WHY THIS RECIPE WORKS

In this nontraditional riff on Bolognese, red lentils create a wonderfully filling sauce that coats orecchiette perfectly. This recipe plays with fall flavors by using a mix of pumpkin puree and tomatoes rather than a tomato-forward sauce. To further play with flavors, we add lightly sweet spices like a touch of ginger and cinnamon. It's certainly not Nonna's Bolognese, but it's a fabulous homage!

SUBSTITUTIONS

Orecchiette: Tagliatelle or pappardelle
Pumpkin puree: Tomato puree or sweet potato puree
Pumpkin seeds: Crushed pecans or slivered almonds

EQUIPMENT & LEFTOVERS

You'll need: Wide pot, large pot, colander, and small skillet
Leftovers: Store in an airtight container in the fridge for 3 days

INGREDIENTS

1 tablespoon avocado oil

1 yellow onion, peeled and diced

1 teaspoon dry thyme

1 teaspoon garlic powder

½ teaspoon ground ginger

½ teaspoon ground cinnamon

½ teaspoon crushed red pepper

Salt and pepper to taste

2 tablespoons tomato paste

½ cup red lentils

1 (15-ounce) can pumpkin puree

2 cups water

1 (15-ounce) can crushed tomatoes

16 ounces orecchiette

½ cup raw pumpkin seeds

½ cup loosely packed fresh parsley, minced

2 tablespoons extra-virgin olive oil

Flaky sea salt to taste

(Continued on page 196)

METHOD

1. **Prepare the Bolognese:** Heat the avocado oil in a wide pot over medium heat. Add the onion and cook for 10 minutes until it softens and begins to turn golden brown. Add the thyme, garlic powder, ginger, cinnamon, and crushed red pepper and cook for 1 minute until fragrant. Season the aromatics with salt and pepper. Add the tomato paste and stir to coat the onions in the paste. Cook for 1 to 2 minutes until the pasta deepens in color. Add the red lentils and cook for 1 minute.

2. **Simmer the Bolognese:** Add the pumpkin puree, water, and crushed tomatoes to the pot. Bring to a boil, then cover, reduce the heat, and simmer for 45 minutes until the lentils are very tender. Stir the lentils occasionally and add a splash of water to loosen them up if the liquid cooks off too quickly. Taste and season with salt and pepper.

3. **Cook the pasta:** Bring a large pot of salted water to a boil. Cook the orecchiette until al dente. Reserve ¼ cup of the pasta water. Drain the pasta and set aside.

4. **Prepare the pumpkin seed garnish:** Place a small skillet on the stovetop over medium heat. Add the pumpkin seeds and toast for 1 to 2 minutes until golden. Turn off the heat and transfer to a bowl. Add the fresh parsley, extra-virgin olive oil, and a pinch of flaky sea salt and toss to combine. Set aside.

5. **Finish the pasta:** Add the cooked pasta to the Bolognese along with the reserved pasta cooking water. Toss until the pasta is completely coated. Turn off the heat.

6. **To serve:** Divide the cooked pasta between bowls and pile the pumpkin seed garnish on top. Enjoy!

Spicy Beans with Mashed Celeriac

Time to Make: 40 minutes (15 minutes inactive)

Serves: 4

WHY THIS RECIPE WORKS

Celeriac is a delightfully aromatic root vegetable that will give you a nice celery flavor to your mash. Served with sweet and spicy beans, this meal is going to make itself right at home in your weekly rotation.

SUBSTITUTIONS

Great northern beans: Your favorite white bean, such as navy, cannellini, or chickpeas
Celeriac: If you cannot find celeriac, replace it with more potatoes or use a root vegetable like turnips, rutabaga, or parsnips

EQUIPMENT & LEFTOVERS

You'll need: Wide pot, medium pot, and potato masher
Leftovers: Store in an airtight container in the fridge for 3 days

INGREDIENTS

1 tablespoon avocado oil

2 shallots, peeled and sliced into wedges

2 teaspoons smoked paprika

2 teaspoons chili powder

1 teaspoon sweet paprika

½ teaspoon cayenne powder or crushed red pepper

1 tablespoon ground white pepper, divided

4 cups vegetable stock

1 tablespoon brown sugar or maple syrup

2 (15-ounce) cans great northern beans

2 scallions, minced, divided

2 pounds celeriac (celery root), peeled and cubed

1 pound (4 whole) Yukon Gold potatoes, peeled and cubed

1¾ teaspoon salt, divided

1 teaspoon garlic powder

½ teaspoon white pepper

¾ cup plant-based sour cream

2 tablespoons plant-based butter

Splash of oat milk, as needed

Black pepper to taste

(Continued on page 199)

METHOD

1. **Sauté the shallots:** Heat the avocado oil in a wide pot over medium heat. Add the shallots and cook for 5 minutes, stirring occasionally, until lightly browned.

2. **Bloom the spices:** Turn the heat to medium-low and add the smoked paprika, chili powder, sweet paprika, cayenne powder or crushed red pepper, and ½ teaspoon white pepper and toss to coat the shallots in the spices. Cook for 1 minute until the spices become fragrant.

3. **Simmer the beans:** Immediately pour in the vegetable stock and bring to a boil. Add the brown sugar or maple syrup and the beans and reduce heat to low. Simmer, uncovered, for 30 minutes. Taste and season to your preferences.

4. **Cook the celeriac and potatoes:** Cover the potatoes and celeriac with water in a medium pot and add 1 teaspoon salt. Bring to a boil and cook for 20 to 30 minutes until fork tender. Drain, then return the cooked potatoes and celeriac to the pot over low heat and add the garlic powder, remaining white pepper, and the plant-based sour cream and use a potato masher to mash until desired texture is reached. Add the plant-based butter and continue mashing until creamy. Add oat milk, if necessary, to thin it out to your desired consistency. Season with remaining salt and the pepper to taste.

5. **Finish the beans:** Right before serving, stir the white parts of the scallions into the beans and cook for 3 to 4 minutes more. Taste and season once more to your preferences. Turn off the heat.

6. **To serve:** Spoon the mashed celeriac into shallow bowls and flatten it with the back of a spoon. Ladle the beans on top and garnish with the reserved scallion greens. Enjoy!

About the Author

Kylie Perrotti is a Baltimore-based, self-taught home cooking enthusiast and art director. She found her passion for cooking as a kid in the kitchen with her parents, and she found her love of food photography when she began photographing for magazines while living in New York City. She started her website triedandtruerecipe.com because she wanted a no-frills, no-nonsense approach to finding easy, elegant, delicious meals to make at home.

After moving back to Baltimore, she expanded her passion for cooking to building community and started the Baltimore Supper Club, a communal and inclusive cooking and food education club in the Baltimore Metro Area whose mission is to connect Baltimore residents over a unified love of cooking. The club is for cooks of all levels who want to enhance their palate and cooking skills through an active and supportive online community, themed dinner parties, and food education events in Baltimore.

Conversion Charts

METRIC AND IMPERIAL CONVERSIONS
(These conversions are rounded for convenience)

Ingredient	Cups/Tablespoons/ Teaspoons	Ounces	Grams/Milliliters
Butter	1 cup/ 16 tablespoons/ 2 sticks	8 ounces	230 grams
Cheese, shredded	1 cup	4 ounces	110 grams
Cream cheese	1 tablespoon	0.5 ounce	14.5 grams
Cornstarch	1 tablespoon	0.3 ounce	8 grams
Flour, all purpose	1 cup/1 tablespoon	4.5 ounces/0.3 ounce	125 grams/8 grams
Flour, whole wheat	1 cup	4 ounces	120 grams
Fruit, dried	1 cup	4 ounces	120 grams
Fruits or veggies, chopped	1 cup	5 to 7 ounces	145 to 200 grams
Fruits or veggies, pureed	1 cup	8.5 ounces	245 grams
Honey, maple syrup, or corn syrup	1 tablespoon	0.75 ounce	20 grams
Liquids: cream, milk, water, or juice	1 cup	8 fluid ounces	240 milliliters
Oats	1 cup	5.5 ounces	150 grams
Salt	1 teaspoon	0.2 ounce	6 grams
Spices: cinnamon, cloves, ginger, or nutmeg (ground)	1 teaspoon	0.2 ounce	5 milliliters
Sugar, brown, firmly packed	1 cup	7 ounces	200 grams
Sugar, white	1 cup/1 tablespoon	7 ounces/0.5 ounce	200 grams/12.5 grams
Vanilla extract	1 teaspoon	0.2 ounce	4 grams

OVEN TEMPERATURES

Fahrenheit	Celsius	Gas Mark
225°	110°	¼
250°	120°	½
275°	140°	1
300°	150°	2
325°	160°	3
350°	180°	4
375°	190°	5
400°	200°	6
425°	220°	7
450°	230°	8

Index

Also Available

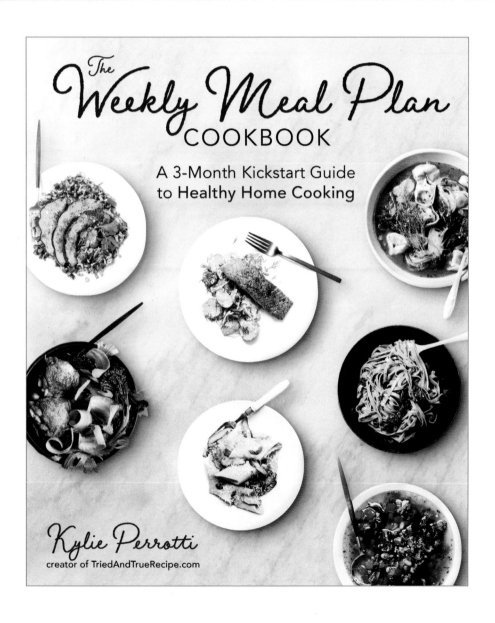